GENADM

G2　　　　1　　　　　ADULT

RICH BOZZETT PRESENTS

SEX, DRUGS AND BON JOVI
(1983 –1989)

OCT 25　1986　8:00PM

Blumberg Corporate Services
62 White Street
New York, New York 10013

Cover design Mike LoPriore
Design and production bobsteimle.com
Printed in the United States of America

First Edition: June 2010

Library of Congress Control Number: 2010908208

ISBN 13: 978-0-9846133-0-4
ISBN 10: 0-9846133-0-7

To the "Unsung Heroes"

Contents

Roseland Ballroom "Listening Party" to kick off New Jersey Syndicate tour in November '88

WANNA BE BON JOVI'S TOUR MANAGER?

18 year old John Bongiovi records "Runaway" with co-writer Jack Ponti and producer Billy Squier

Imagine being fresh out of high school and a two-year stint in the Navy, not knowing what to do with your life, and getting a phone call asking if you'd like to be the tour manager for Bon Jovi. My name is Richard Bozzett, and that's what happened to me on September 24, 1983. And for the next 6 years I toured the world with what would become one of the biggest rock bands of all time as it catapulted from total obscurity to unimaginable superstardom. At the time, I didn't know who Bon Jovi was—and neither did anyone else except for Doc McGhee and Derek Schulman.

Derek was a particularly quick and sharp A&R exec from Polygram who had just signed Jon Bon Jovi to a record contract after his song "Runaway" won a local radio contest. Doc was an up-and-coming band manager who had cultivated a relationship with Derek and was expecting to sign Jon to a personal management contract. It was Doc who called me to offer me the job. When I met him I was his limousine driver.

When you drive people around on a regular basis, you really get to know them— sometimes better than their own families. For example, before he called me that fateful day, I already knew one of Doc's businesses was importing cannabis—pot—and I also knew exactly "why"… Doc used to be a waiter who dreamed of being a rock band manager. He wasn't born into privilege, no one ever gave him anything, and no

Doc and I head off on a business trip in Doc's plane

bank was going to give him a loan. Being a rock band manager is a big dream that costs big money— because you can't sign a band that has any potential and keep them working long enough to become stars without first having a lot of it. So Doc got involved in the pot business to get his hands on enough money to get into the rock and roll business. I couldn't tell you how much pot he had a hand in importing or selling, but one shipment for which he was busted carried 20 tons—40,000 pounds: enough to fill the hull of a freighter. So this was a guy with some very big dreams.

While most other managers would flaunt their big-name acts and the number of platinum albums under their belts, or promise year-long tours to win over new talent, Doc had no track record, so he had to take another tack. HIS formula for convincing talent to sign with him instead of going with better-established managers already in the business was simply this: "I'm smart, I'll give you personal attention, AND there's a hell of a party going on right now down at my place in Miami that you don't want to miss!" Doc's appeal to aspiring artists was emotional. He convinced them that he that would make them rock stars by treating them like they already were rock stars—and that took a shitload of money. He had just recently used that strategy to sign Mötley Crüe, the insanely hot California party band, and he was now using it to do the same with Bon Jovi.

Jon was about ready to sign with Doc—only there was a turd in the punchbowl. While Doc was away for a few days in Florida, famed promoter John Scher booked Bon Jovi to open for ZZ Top at Madison Square Garden—and Doc couldn't get back to New York in time to

Richie plays "Runaway" solo
at Madison Square Garden

be there. Doc was concerned Scher would try to make a move on Jon and sign him while he was away, so he called me to represent him at the Garden so that Scher would see Doc's guys were there and stand down.

I had no experience as a band manager, but I did a short stint as a valet for the first band Doc signed, Pat Travers, that proved I had the requisite problem-solving skills needed for the job. Pat Travers was the opening act for Aerosmith during their 'Black Pearl' tour. And when Steven Tyler overdosed in Pat Travers' hotel room at the end of the tour, I was the guy who called for help and threw him into a cold shower long enough to keep him conscious until the medics arrived.

I had become Doc's go-to guy, so when he called to ask me to cover for him, I told him I'd be there.

It was already late on Saturday afternoon when Doc called. I took a shower and drove with my girlfriend Patti from Long Island into the city. I arrived at Madison Square Garden just in time. It was a little like that scene in the Godfather when Michael arrives at the hospital to discover the crooked cop has booted his father's body guards out of there in order to finish him off, and I was the 'baker' recruited by Michael at the last minute to look like a body guard in order to hold off the expected assault. I had to rise to the occasion and play the part.

I knew this was going to be the first time the band would play a 20,000 seat venue, and that Jon would be on edge. When we met, Jon was already justifiably upset because his lights and sound system weren't working. He had a guest list of 150 people but was well aware that what was at stake went well beyond the impression he would make that night with 150 family and friends. A screw-up THIS early in his career could derail it, or set the wrong tone for the whole future. So I went about the job of trying to manage his guest list while finding someone who could help us resolve the technical issues. I tracked down ZZ Top's sound and light crew because Jon didn't have light and sound people. That was a good call because, as I would later learn, the light and sound for an opening act is always under the technical supervision of the headlining act, and at that point, no one in the headlining crew had any idea anything was wrong on their end. I reassured Jon that everything would be taken care of and then just held my breath and tried to stay calm in order to keep him calm.

As the crew began troubleshooting the problem, I just stood there with Jon, on the stage, in the dark, listening to the murmur of the increasingly impatient crowd stirring all around us. I had my arm around him, trying to keep him calm, and I could feel his heart racing. But at this point, it was out of our hands. After considerable time and effort, ZZ Top's crew restored light and power—and as the lights and power came on, so did that trademark smile on Jon's face. I hadn't yet heard Jon sing or the band play, but just by the look on Jon's face I knew that this was what he was meant to do. I figured the best way for me to help Jon concentrate on being Jon onstage would be by taking care of everything else. At that moment I understood what a tour manager does. I had written the first paragraph of my own job description—a job description that would guide me for years to come.

There was just enough time to salvage "Runaway" and a few other songs in the Bon Jovi set. It ended up being a great show and Bon Jovi's arena debut was a success. Best of all, the next day Doc was back in town to sign him. I was officially Bon Jovi's tour manager, and moving on to the most improbable journey of a lifetime.

Backstage after first gig opening for ZZ Top at Madison Square Garden

Enjoying a rare day off on tour

THE "ADMIRAL"

As with any job, there is a "big picture" to being a tour manager. Putting on live shows, touring, is the lifeblood of any band…particularly a new band, because that's how you build a base of fans. Live shows create excitement and radio play, and that attracts new people who buy tickets, records and merchandise/t-shirts.

So what does a tour manager do? There isn't a formal job description, but I think the best way of summing it up is this: it's like being "Nicky" in the movie Casino, with Jon as Sam Rothstein and Doc McGhee as Remo. The tour manager has to make sure all is well with the band and that nothing gets screwed up so that the band can concentrate on performing and making money for the boys back home. McGhee Entertainment, Bon Jovi's management company, earned 20% of everything Bon Jovi made—records, tickets, merchandise. When there's that much money involved, somebody has to be made accountable for making sure every minute of time translates into money. It is, after all, a business. And the idea is to try to turn it into a HUGE business.

Advancing next day's show
and travel arrangements

The basic job is to see to it that the band, crew and equipment arrives at every venue on time and that the band members have their personal and professional needs met so they can concentrate on giving the best show they can. We're not talking about a bunch of prima donnas who need someone to follow them around with a glass of orange juice. We're talking about 5 guys who are literally living in a bus and working at breakneck pace to become stars by putting on 200+ live shows a year. You have to get a doctor or an ambulance when someone keels over with heat exhaustion or needs 30 stitches after getting his head split open. You have to make sure there are no slip-ups with the venue, the hotel or travel arrangements, manage local radio and promotion, prepare the band and accompany them to every business meeting, book and attend radio and TV interviews and promotional events, and decide who the band can meet and greet before and after each show. And you have to make sure the band gets paid.

But the tour manager is also the "fixer", the "problem solver" for anything and everything that could possibly go wrong or anything that's needed when you're on a tour. For example, say the gig is in Australia but the equipment was accidentally sent to some guy named Sydney. The tour manager has to make a shitload of phone calls and call in a lot of favors to find guitars, amps, and microphones and get them to the venue before the show.

After the show is over, you have to get the band out of the venue and either back to the hotel or to the bus or plane that's taking you to tomorrow's show. You eat every meal with the band, sleep and travel with the band, do every interview with and party with the band.

When it's time to leave one town to head to another and the weather sucks, the tour manager

Backstage looking after the band and the guest list

Brothers for life

has to decide whether to cancel a show or put the whole band onto a plane that could end up doing the Buddy Holly dance. Ground the plane, and you're the pussy who cancelled the gig and cost us a ton of money. Let it fly, and you're the reckless asshole who didn't know what he was doing and nearly killed everybody. Every day is filled with new, unanticipated problems, and it seems the same problem never happens twice.

The worst problems are the ones that are unnecessary and totally avoidable—the ones someone on your own team brought on all by himself out of carelessness or out of sheer stupidity. These are the ones that'll cost you the whole day to sort out…like how to get your lighting director out of jail after he gets arrested for making bomb jokes while on a security line on his way to board a plane to the next gig; or who do you get to play bass when Alec is wasted and fails to show up; or what do you do when Jon comes down with a case of the crabs on the last day of the tour, is headed directly home, and you can't get meds. It doesn't stop—for at least a year at a time. It's a little like being the principal of a middle school where they serve beer.

Sometimes the job is about quietly exercising a little common sense to keep everybody out of trouble. For example, you have to make sure no one brings any "guests" on the bus

You work 24/7 every day—for about a year at a time

because you can't run the risk of dragging some 20-year old nymphomaniac across state lines when she is actually only 15. At the same time, if one of the guys in the band DOES invite some girl to come with us from Philadelphia to Buffalo for example, you've got to make sure she isn't underage and that she gets back safely to Philadelphia the next day without making a big deal out of it.

Looking for a little down time? 'Tour Manager' isn't for you…

You handle the guests, cover all the interviews and business meetings and attend all the shows and functions. Yes, some of it is "glamorous," but just like ANY job, most of it isn't glamorous at all. When the show is over and the audience heads home to their warm beds, you're coordinating all the logistics for the next 24 hours while the band showers in some cold backstage bathroom before heading off to a bus, a plane, or a hotel carrying a bag with a few personal items in tow.

And by the way, this was the 80's and there weren't any cell phones, so you had to make sure that your pre-planning was rock-solid. Otherwise, 6 very tired guys in need of sleep could be standing around in some hotel lobby that has no rooms.

You've got to be "on" all the time, because you work from the time you wake up until the time you go to bed. On off-days you go out with the band to see the sights, so you never really just do nothing and recharge the batteries. That comes between tours. And you could wait a year or more to do that.

The tour manager is also the liaison to the boys back home, the label, and the management company. Just like with the band, you're on call with them every minute of the time you're on

Richie and Jon when they were just a couple of guys with a dream

the road. And the "Runaway" tour was 14 months long, the "7800" tour was 11 months long, and the "Slippery When Wet" tour was 15 months long. Because it's a 24-hour a day job, one year on the road is the equivalent of three years at a regular job with regular hours.

It's not the kind of job where you can have a balanced life—you know: work time, family time, personal time. Everyone is 100% consumed with 'work' 24/7. You do it because you want to help the band achieve their dreams and enjoy the economic rewards downstream.

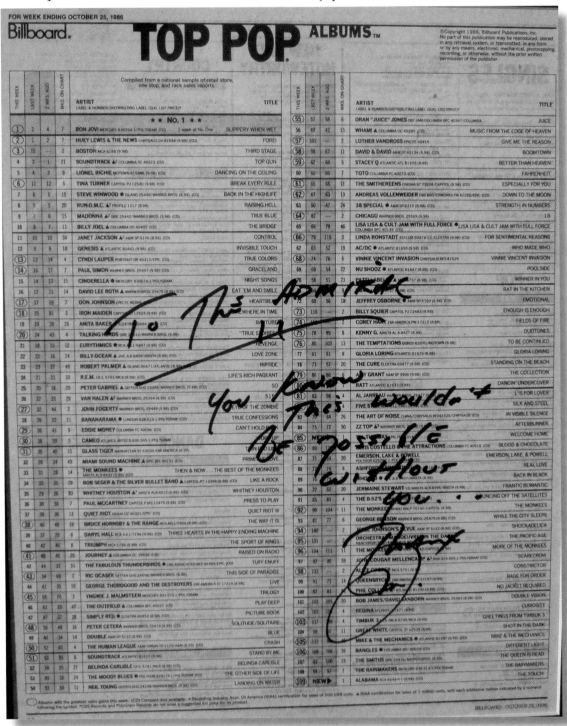

Recognition is its own reward

Their dreams become your dreams. Anyone who goes on tour with a band sacrifices the most anyone can sacrifice and makes as big a bet as anyone can make. They bet themselves on their band. In the meantime, the only saving grace is you can share the life with others by bringing them along some of the time; but eventually even that novelty wears off, so in many respects, it's a race against time. Only the people inside the circle truly understand that.

Inside the circle I was #7 (behind Jon, the band and Doc who were numbers 1-6), and called "The Admiral"—a term affectionately bestowed on me by Richie Sambora and instantly adopted by the rest of the band. Richie was #2 and called "The King of Swing," based not only on his musical virtuosity as many people think, but on his physical endowment. My nickname refers to being the go-to guy for the band, and handling all the issues, problems and details with military precision.

The open tour book below shows the schedule and details for a single show on the right side, and my notes and additions to the guest list on the left. Add to this everything that can go wrong and the fact that I did this for 4 tours and over 1,400 shows and you begin to get the idea of what it's like to be the tour manager.

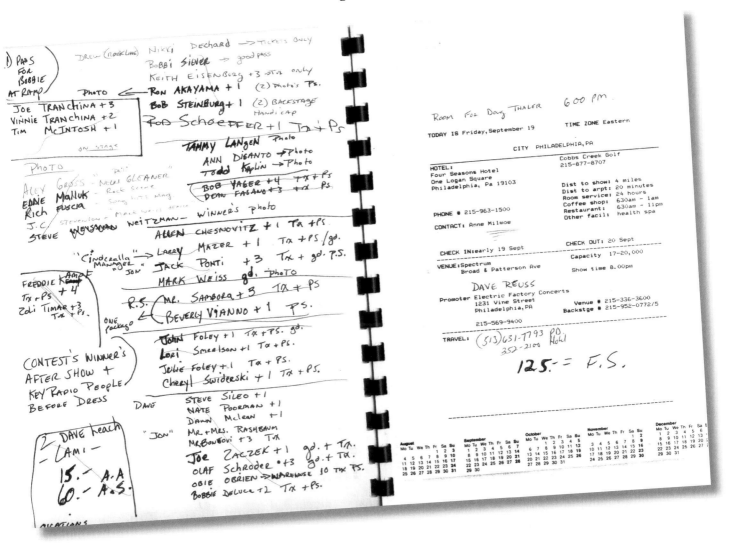

During the 80's there wasn't any such thing as e-mail, so the home office used to contact me on the road by sending a "TELEX" to my hotel:

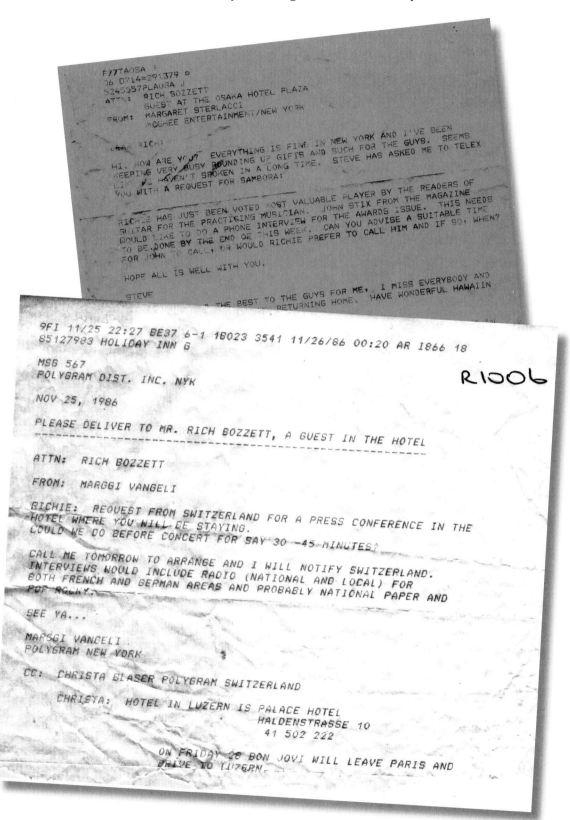

B.J. 10/16

GOING ON THE ROAD

When you first go out on the road, it's as an "opening act" for an established band as a way of building a fan base of your own. Once you've built up a significant number of fans to whom to sell records, tickets and merchandise, the label and management company are more willing to invest money in the band and the show; and there is a greater likelihood of the band actually making it. That said, one of the biggest benefits of going on the road is that it gives you the endurance to back up your desires. The experience either turns you into the actual performing artist you already thought you were, or makes you quit and stop wasting your time.

Bon Jovi in 1983 performing in Philadelphia where their first two albums were recorded

Our first time out on the road was the second week in October 1983, when the band opened four shows for Eddie Money. Polygram hadn't put out Bon Jovi's record yet, and there wasn't a tour schedule or budget yet, so this was real seat-of-the-pants shit.

It was Jon, Richie, Alec, Tico , David and I with all our clothes and luggage in my dad's station wagon, and the equipment in tow in a U-haul trailer, driving to four cities in four days. I stayed over at Jon's house the night before we left so we wouldn't be late. Jon's mom Carol treated me like one of the family.

She put me up in Jon's brother Tony's room and made a big dinner that night and a huge breakfast buffet the next morning. That's just the way Jon's mom was—she treated everyone like family. His dad, John, a hair dresser, was a great person too, but he was a lot more easy-going, whereas Carol was more goal-oriented. Both of them encouraged Jon to pursue his dreams, but there's no question in my mind that he got his ambition from mom, and his personable charm from dad.

I hardly slept that night because I was so excited. As far as Jon and I were concerned, making it was never a question. Naively, we believed that as long as the band was performing, it was on its way to stardom. The band had a great first record in "Runaway." And the energy captured in that studio recording powered the reputation of the live performance of the band as an opening act instantly, and still holds up to this day. On our way out the door, Jon's dad took me aside and said, "Rich, take care of my boy for me" —and I told him I would.

We were playing for exposure, not for money. At that time, anybody could pick up the phone and book Bon Jovi for $180-$250 a night. Today, you'd be hard-pressed to buy a ticket for that price. We all had to share one hotel room, so my dad's car became the hangout of choice where the guys took the girls before, during and after the shows. I used to worry about somebody breaking into the U-Haul and taking the equipment, so I'd get up during the night and look out the window to check on it. It was easy to spot, even in a parking lot crowded with campers and trucks. I would just look for the one rocking back and forth.

I quickly came to understand what life on the road would be like. All that driving in such a short period of time took a serious toll on me. I remember being so tired near the end of the four days that I couldn't drive the 380 miles to the last show in Erie, Pa., so Alec gave me some kind of speed/amphetamine to make sure I didn't fall asleep behind the wheel and kill us all. I remember puking my guts out when we finally got there because I wasn't used to taking speed to get amped up. But it was exactly what I needed that night to keep us alive. Problem was, when the show was over and it was time to go, I was completely toasted, and so was everyone else but Alec. He looked wide awake, bright eyed and bushy-tailed. He said, "give me the keys. I'll drive,", and I said, "By all means, you drive." Everyone was out like a light, but we all woke up at the same time as Alec pulled up to the hotel in Philadelphia, still looking bright-eyed and bushy-tailed, and announced "We're here!" Alec loved the life. He loved it so much he never

Ray brought a musician's point of view to the business

slept. I always admired how he was such a great theatrical performer—the third "mobile" player on the stage—and the perfect complement to Jon and Richie. The man had a real persona. He was frequently overshadowed in the press by Jon and Richie, but he fit the two of them like a glove and complemented their style the way George Harrison did for Lennon

Julie Foley made the office run like clockwork

and McCartney. He also rounded out the vocals with a powerful voice that was way the hell up there, always in pitch, and in every way on the same level as Jon's and Richie's.

While we were on the road, back in New York they were working on a plan for the image of the band. Everyone had a different opinion about what the band should be called and how the music should sound—even whether the band should be pop, rock, or metal. Ray Ovetsky from McGhee Entertainment hired a marketing positioning expert from Young & Rubicam (Y&R), Jordan Stanley, to help sort through all the marketing issues and devise an objective, data-based direction. Ray was a Julliard-trained musician who brought a musician's perspective to the company. Ray and office manager Julie Foley were among the first employees to join McGhee Entertainment. Originally the sound engineer for Doc's first band, Pat Travers, Ray worked out of McGhee Entertainment's NY office at 240 Central Park South, putting together the incredibly detailed equipment manifests required to actually put both Mötley Crüe and Bon Jovi on the road.

In 1983, you could book Bon Jovi for $250

Ray, Derek, Doc and Jordan compiled a list of all the open issues, and used focus groups and one-on-one interviews with teen females 14-17 and teen males and females 18-20, to sort through all of them. It was one of the first times consumer research was used that way in the music business. They basically allowed the audience to settle all the open issues by listening to the band's music. Getting input directly from girls who buy records was much more valuable to Jon than arbitrary feedback from other sources, particularly when there was so much conflicting and contradictory input coming from within the Management Company and record label.

The marketing research team rented a van and played the songs from the band's first album for teen record buyers as they exited record stores in malls in Valley Stream and Massapequa, NY. Then they surveyed the kids about who they thought the band was, where they were from, and what they were like, and what their favorite songs were and "why"—all based on the music the band created. Then they showed photographs of the band members

At a time when most rockers just stood around on stage, Bon Jovi was more athletic and energetic

and asked the kids who they liked and why, etc. It was the same kind of research companies use to build brands.

A key difference between Bon Jovi and all the older bands in the business (like the Stones who were #1 at the time) was the fact that they were kids playing for kids rather than 50 year olds playing for their dads. The guys were "athletic" and "energetic" long before that became fashionable in music. It was the dawn of wireless, freeing performers to move around more on the stage unencumbered by wires; so Jordan thought it was important for the band to bring a lot of raw energy to the show and put a lot of movement on the stage. No one else was doing that in 1983, and kids LOVED

John's energy, hair and smile were his strongest assets

it. I think in some way, it was the high-energy performance of 80's bands like Bon Jovi that spawned the gymnastics-driven pop-musical groups and solo acts that sprung up throughout the 90's and which continue to dominate pop culture today. From the initial research emerged the positioning of Jon and Richie as front men and co-writing team; with Jon truly embracing instead of questioning his identity as a very young, lively and energetic hard rock band and front man with Jersey/Italian roots; and once and for all, it marked the end of the ongoing debate over whether or not to change the band's name from Bon Jovi to something else.

Pam Maher, a friend of Mötley tour manager Richie Fisher, had been suggesting that the band use the name Bon Jovi, but no one in the inner circle was excited about it. The issue of what name to use remained open for months, until the research quietly and uneventfully put the matter to rest. Kids of all age groups thought the name was cool, and it was easier to remember

Richie's good looks and charisma made him a fan favorite

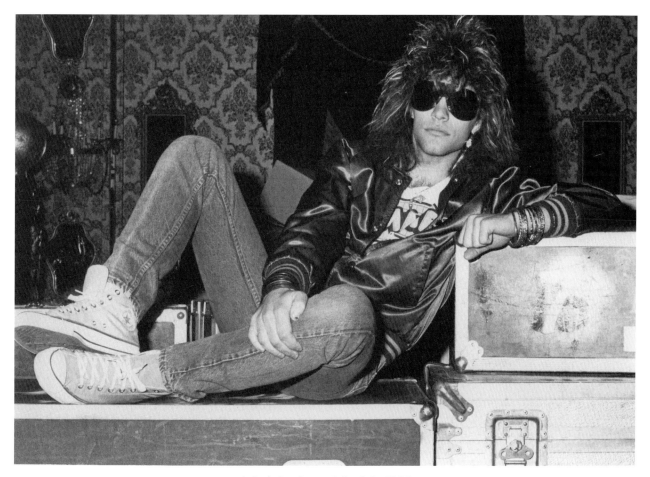

John's trademark look in 1983

and pronounce than the original Bongiovi. Looking back, it's hard to imagine there was ever a debate about the name in the first place, but then again, everything is always crystal clear in hindsight.

What girls loved most about Jon were his teeth and hair, and Jon and his team went to work with that to create his trademark early 80's look. It was a Y&R art director named Lisa Llewelyn who came up with the idea of highlighting Jon's hair to give him a "cherubic" look—a look which, once perfected, quite literally rendered girls helpless just by looking at him.

The band appealed to a very young and female audience—and in order to achieve the critical mass required to become a headliner, Bon Jovi would have to broaden the lyrical content of its songs and harden the rock and roll edge of its sound to appeal to older males and females. Thus, the first rounds of research put in motion a blueprint that would be followed for the next three years. When the debut album was released, we were all put on a salary of $250 per week and it was time to start the "Runaway" tour. That figure was for everyone—Jon made $250 per week, as did I, and every member of the band and the crew. We were ecstatic—hell, we were getting paid to do what we loved, and if the band made it, everyone knew they would be along for the long run.

The band about to leave for Japan to begin the "Runaway" tour

THE RUNAWAY TOUR

The album was released January 25, 1984 and we set out on the road to support it on the "Runaway" tour starting April 9, 1984. Opening for the Scorpions, the first leg of the tour went from April 9 until the end of July. The second leg of the tour took us to the UK and Europe from the end of September through early November, opening for Kiss. In between, the band did some TV appearances, including "American Bandstand."

Now, for the first time, we were really on the road as an opening act—playing everyday, traveling everyday, and best of all, playing 20,000 seat arenas instead of 3000 seat venues. When you start to play arenas, you give up the intimacy of a club for a taste of the excitement stardom holds. There are new challenges to the band's stamina because there's more real estate

First Day on Tour!
"Were Tired" 4/10/84

to cover—both onstage and geographically. There's more exposure, greater media coverage, and the stakes are higher. You're in the right place, a tangible step closer to the stardom you seek, but you're not yet headlining. But as an "opening act," you start to see what it's like to be the headlining act. And we had the best headlining act anyone could hope to have first time out of the gate—the Scorpions.

The Scorpions were an older and more seasoned German band. At a time when Jon and I were 20 and 21, Klaus Meine and Rudolf Schenker were 36 years old and had 14 albums under their belts. These guys knew what they were doing; they had a whole lot of records and a fan base that wasn't fickle. And in 1984, I'd have to say, these guys were in their prime.

Looking back, surely this was the time Bon Jovi really started playing at the level at which stars have to play everyday. And the Scorpions set a high bar for performance. I think we were extremely fortunate to have them as our first headlining act, because they infused in the band a style and set of standards

Klaus Meine arrives as Richie plays cards with Rudy Schenker and Matthias Jabs from Scorpions

that was definitely at the high end of the range. And there wasn't the slightest bit of ego crap going on. These guys were great and they knew it. But they had no illusions about it...and no exaggerated sense of self-importance because of it. They had fun at it because they were good at it. Nice. And I think that's what made them good role models for the band. Opening for the Scorpions gave the whole Bon Jovi band a role model for stage performance that they would emulate, make their own, and later, surpass. Even as you listen today to the guitar solos of Richie Sambora, you can hear a little Matthias Jabs. And when I hear the vocal perfection of Jon Bon Jovi I can hear a little Klaus Meine.

Playing arenas is a lot different from bars and clubs, even for an opening act. There's a lot more stage to cover and a lot more audience to interact with. Plus, the schedule is grueling—one date right after another. That's a lot different from doing four dates and taking a week off. On the "Runaway" tour we traded my dad's station wagon for a tour bus—then two tour buses.

Our first bus—with driver Bill "Gator" Mosley... Gator brought along his huge gun collection

The band and I traveled on one bus, the crew and production manager on the other. Most of the traveling is done during the night, after a show. On a typical show day, we would be up before noon, and I would take Jon to do radio and promo interviews. We'd come back for a sound check and dinner, meet with guests from the label and then get cranked up for the show.

Richie's guitars all tuned up and ready to go in order of how he will use them

There's nothing quite like the time just before the show. The sun's going down and you feel the energy of the crowd building up and your heart racing. Showtime's an explosion of raw energy, but after the show you're still amped up and headed out to the next venue. So it's a quick shower at the venue and onto the bus, where you try to sleep or at least rest while you drive all night to the next city and the next show. Jon and I took the two beds opposite each other in the middle of the bus so we could hit the meetings and interviews the next day without waking everybody up. Sometimes we'd hit a truck stop for gas and something to eat before going to bed. Whoever's up and hungry gets off and eats. Whoever's in bed sleeps through.

On one trip from Atlanta down to St. Petersburg, Florida, we accidentally left Alec back

America runs on Dunkin but our bus ran on Dunkin, gas and cocaine

at the diner before driving 40 miles and realizing he wasn't there. We circled back to find him lying down in front of the diner, happily resting on something that wasn't moving as he waited for us to return. After that episode, I had the guys leave their tour passes on the bus' steering wheel whenever they left the bus so we would know who was and who wasn't onboard.

Jon reads off the breakfast specials while blind-folded by sugar packets

If we pulled into town a little before the show, we'd check into a hotel and get three rooms—one for the bus driver, one for whoever wanted to sleep, and one room to use to shower and change. Jon and I were

Inside the circle, Alec was called "Alec the Cat" because he never slept

usually on a different schedule from the band because Jon would do all the promotion interviews and meetings, and I would accompany him to all of them. All the guys appreciated what was no more than just a nice clean Holiday Inn room. It was so much better than sleeping on the bus. We'd be up by noon and do it all over again. Usually five or six shows a week, for more than a year at a time.

What made things especially challenging for the band was the fact that Doc tried to book the band every single day in order to get back the money that he was hemorrhaging by keeping them on the road—about a million dollars a year. Playing everyday helped offset the losses and keep the band in the news, but I argued with Doc that it was putting Jon's voice on the edge especially with Jon also promoting shows, doing radio interviews, and doing magazine interviews all day every day. We brought onboard Don Lawrence and Katie Agresta, two of the very best vocal coaches in the

The Holiday Inn seemed like the Ritz Carlton

business, to help Jon strengthen his voice so he could do two hour shows 5-6 days a week instead of having his voice melt down after twenty minutes. Jon had a great work ethic and never missed his practice, warm ups or vocalizing down exercises after the show.

There are a lot of frustrations that go along with being an opening act. As an "opening act" the basic idea is to just get the audience warmed up enough to really rock when the headliner comes on—but not to steal the show. You have a very small fan base, little budget to work with, one shared dressing room (compared to the headline act that gets separate dressing rooms), limited sound and lights (paid for by the label but on loan from the headlining act), and when you fly, even for 20 hours to the other side of the world, you go coach. If you use too much of the stage or too much light, play a little too loud or too long, you're going to catch hell from the headlining act—and for good reason. Typically, the opening act is allotted 25 minutes. Bon Jovi always went 27-35 minutes, and that would create trouble. The problem is that most venues are union buildings and if you're five minutes over in a union building on the opening act's set, you're going to be at LEAST that at 11 o'clock when the gig is officially over, and then you go into overtime. And if you're overtime at 11, you've got to pay 70 guys another $65 an hour (almost $5 grand every night, every time it happens), and that money comes out of the headlining band's pocket. If that happens 6 nights a week it really adds up to very serious money.

Tico hitches a ride to the room with Alec on hotel luggage cart

David, Jon and Richie have a snooze on the long flight to Japan

Jon would normally exceed his allotted show time because he got into it and left it all on the stage. So it was a pretty regular occurrence for the headlining act's tour manager to go off on me TWICE every night. Once in front of MY band to let them know not to do it, and once in front of THEIR band so they knew he told us not to do it. The headlining band's tour manager isn't going to talk directly to Jon and the band—hell, these guys are up-and-coming stars and he might have to work for them someday. So he's going to scream at me within earshot of the band as a way of talking to the band without screaming directly at them. It would happen like clockwork every night. No sooner would I get back to the dressing room after a show than the Scorpions' tour manager, Bob Adcock, would show up to give me an earful—something like, "Dude, you got to get off the stage—I just got my ass fuckin' reamed again, and the next time it happens I'm turning on the house lights and there'll be no passes tomorrow!!"

Then he'd get me a second time in front of HIS band to let HIS guys know he was doing his job and watching out for their wallet for them. It would be like, "Richie, I do everything for you, and you fuck me! The next time I'm turning on the fuckin' house lights. This fuckin' horseshit is going to stop! No passes tomorrow night!" The funny thing was, Bob was actually gay, so when I came back after getting a "reaming," everybody in the band would ask me how deep it went and how sore my ass was—very funny!

Our crew, sympathetic to my ongoing plight and increasingly sore ass, came to be known as "the minutemen" because they could get us on and off as an opening act in one minute. That way Jon could have more time on stage, and my ass would be little less sore. I'd like to be able to take credit for what the minutemen did, but the thing is, they took that initiative on their own because they didn't want to see me get reamed and didn't want to force Jon to cut down on his stage time. Tell me where you'd expect to find a crew that thought like that and did what they were able to do. We had such an incredible team because everyone took initiatives to make the whole machine work better. These days, they write books about how to do that. Back then, guys did it all on instinct and out of their pride of ownership. But regardless of how well we all worked

Jon left it all on the stage—ANYTHING for the audience

You can't argue with anyone when you can't feel your tongue

together, as an opening act we were constantly on the defensive with the headliner, and we had very little or nothing to negotiate with.

Whenever tensions started running too hot, I'd get on the phone and call Doc, who would get on a plane with as much pot and cocaine as he could carry and fly to meet us wherever we were going to be the next day. Then, as the band took the stage as the opening act, Doc would call a "management meeting" with all disgruntled parties, and the meeting didn't start until everyone did a couple lines. One way or another, those management meetings had the effect of reconciling all the issues and resetting everyone back to zero for awhile. When the 'opening act' tensions were under control, all was well. Girls began stalking the band, and one of my jobs was to scout the talent and select a few to come backstage. Richie Fisher used to use code cards to make it fast and easy to get Mötley what they needed. For example,

Richie Fisher was #1, Nicki was #6, "Pigs with lipstick" was #12 (that would be girls who just wanted to blow the band); "Bimbos" was #11 (that would be girls who were exceptionally nice to look at). Krell was #8, and #8 was cocaine. So if after the show you overheard a conversation over the walkie-talkies saying "One, this is 6, need 8 and 11" it meant Nickie was calling Richie to bring bimbos and cocaine to his dressing room.

But Bon Jovi was all-business. Sure there were amphetamines to get amped up before a show, and increasingly, wine and barbiturates to come down afterwards, and Halcion and Valium to sleep. You can't put on a high-energy show any other way, or sleeping is impossible.

There was a lot of pot and cocaine around that the crew, management, sponsors and guests went through. But with the band, the focus was on putting on a great show. You do party with people because that's ultimately what you're selling and what they're buying— total escape from their everyday lives. But no one ever goes on stage in less than total performance mode.

Without the adulation of screaming girls there's really no point in any of it. You want girls backstage for fun, entertainment and to give them a thrill—and you want to let them feel a little of what you're feeling. Crew members routinely gave passes to girls they want to take back to the bus. Our security guards recruited girls for the band. But I was usually too busy managing the guest list, closing out the accounting, and advancing the next morning's arrangements to have anyone backstage.

When a guy thinks with his dick, he knows he will make one bad judgment after another to get what his dick dictates. That's

1. Richie	7. Mary
2. Doug	8. Krell
3. Vince	9. JD
4. Tommy	10. Pigs n pairs
5. Mick	11. Bimbos
6. Nikki	12. Pigs lipstick

Actual Mötley code card with original stains

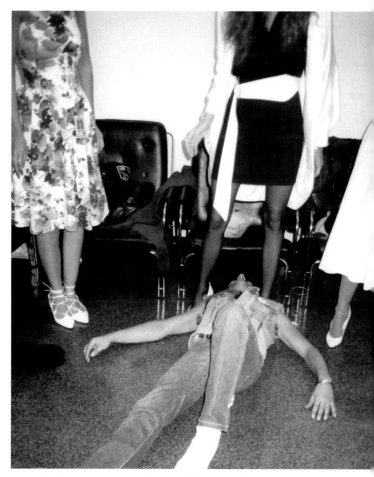

Alec screens candidates for backstage passes

Tico's gets last-minute wardrobe help from Nancy Spencer before taking the stage

the cruel trick nature programmed into him to insure the procreation of our species. So one night when we were staying over in Oklahoma City, and there wasn't too long a guest list and no radio or promo people had to being escorted to meet the band, I gave a backstage pass to an irresistibly sweet-looking thing.

She came backstage and hung out and then invited me over to her place afterwards, which sounded like a perfect way to spend the night. She had a nice new condo with a pool, so we partied for a while at her place and went down to spend the rest of the nice, hot humid night in the built-in pool. Well, just as I was really starting to relax, I looked up and I was staring down the barrel of a fully loaded .44 with what appeared to be an angry boyfriend on the other end, trembling, telling me I'm a dead man. The girl jumped up to chill this guy out, and I took the opportunity to jump out and head back to get my clothes, bag and car keys. And if I just had my keys, I'm pretty sure I would have passed on the clothes and bag and just headed directly to my car. All I could hear was her telling him, "Go, go—I'll get him out; we'll talk about this tomorrow," but he wasn't saying a word and I was pretty sure this was going to be over a lot sooner than later. I recognized that guy's trembling hand. But I definitely dodged a bullet and there wasn't any gunfire.

Girls can make you crazy, and when it comes to rock and roll it's even crazier. I'm telling you that a girl enamored with a band at a rock concert will abandon her husband, boyfriend, childhood sweet-heart or infant child—give away her car, sell her kid sister into slavery or blow a perfect stranger just to get backstage with the band.

I can't tell you the number of times guys have come up to me at the end of concerts looking for their girlfriends who got a chance to go backstage for a few minutes—two hours ago. Girls spend their whole lives trying to keep guys from acting like dogs, even though nature programmed them to act like dogs. Yet girls get exposed to celebrity once and fold like a card table. I don't get it. Never will.

When girls started following the band from the venues to the hotels we had to start using aliases to check into hotels. I would register Jon as Harry Callahan (from Dirty Harry), Tony Montana or

Bon Jovi built a reputation for attracting the prettiest girls

Captain Kidd, Richie as Billy Ray Valentine (from Trading Places), David as Jason Voorhees (from Friday the 13th), Tico as Coco Lopez (from the popular drink),and Alec as Freddy Krueger (Nightmare on Elm Street). I would take a room next to the elevators so I could hear the elevator bell and check out who was coming and going.

The guys preferred hotels, but I have to say I preferred sleeping on the bus while driving through the night because nobody was coming and going. But one night after a concert, in the middle of the night, as we were on the bus driving from St. Louis to Oklahoma City, I awoke in a panic to the sounds of loud, rapid gunfire. The bus was stopped on the side of the road, and I jumped out of bed in my underwear and ran outside to see what was going on. There, on the side of the road, in the middle of the night, in the middle of nowhere, was the band and the bus driver with all kinds of firearms—shotguns, machine guns, hand guns, rifles—shooting up a storm and littering the road and shoulder with shell casings, just blowing off steam. Our driver, Bill "Gator" Mosley, was an ex-cop and collector of all kinds of handguns and automatic weapons, and he and the band decided to try them out in the middle of Missouri in the middle of the night. I told everybody to "stop" and pointed at the headlights of what turned out of be a truck coming from the other direction—miles down the straightaway. I said, "Guys, you can't be shooting off guns in the middle of the night when you have a bus full of pot and cocaine and who knows what else onboard. People are coming, and we have to get out of here. And I'm still not sure we aren't going to get pulled over and arrested!" Everybody looked at me like I was the bitchy neighbor who keeps your ball when it lands on his lawn. But I probably kept us all out of jail that night. And you just can't take the chance of getting arrested or missing a show—especially when you're just getting started.

On July 11, Richie Sambora's birthday, I planted a bag of powdered sugar in his hotel room with a note that said 'happy birthday' and walked him back to his room at the end of the show. I had it all timed so that a stripper in a police uniform would show up pounding on the door a minute after we arrived--and that she would catch us with the bag in hand.

Richie thinks he's been arrested

Richie is happy to find out he's been "punked"

As planned, the girl busted in, handcuffed both of us and took a Polaroid of the scared shitless look on his face before stripping down and singing happy birthday to him. Once he knew what was going on, I took a second Polaroid of him and the girl. Needless to say, Richie was very happy to know that he had been set-up. And he learned what it felt like to be arrested…Later that day he would tell me I was the big brother he never had.

We worked as hard as we played. Believing that the "bigger" you are, the more "thrilling" the experience becomes for the audience AND us. So every night, without exception, we would videotape the whole show, and we would watch it when it was over to see what was working, what wasn't, and what could be improved.

By the end of July, the U.S. "Runaway" tour had wound down, and we had some time off to do some TV appearances including "American Bandstand" before heading off to Europe to open for Kiss in September.

My girlfriend Patti O'Connor was a bank loan officer who was able to work her own hours. So when we got the chance to tour the world together, her schedule was flexible enough to take advantage of it. Patti and Jon's girlfriend, Dorothea, hit it off and became best friends. So when I couldn't be with her, because I was with Jon, she and Dorothea were perfect company for one another.

Opening for Kiss was rock and roll on another level. These guys were the quintessential big league American rock band and I expected to see the drugs and women everywhere. But they were even more "all-business" than Bon Jovi. They worked hard, took off the makeup and went home. That was it.

When we first arrived in the UK, we were traveling with Kiss and staying in the same hotels—until we got to Ipswich. There, we had a wild party in one of our hotel rooms—I'm not sure whose room it was. And after I left, the

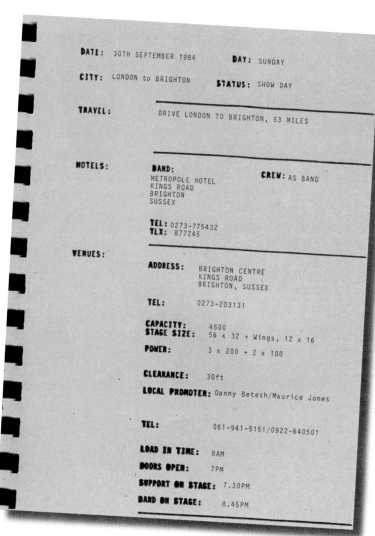

Every tour has a tour book showing the details for each show

guys trashed the room. When it was time to check out, the hotel manager presented me with a bill for damages of 2500£, around $4000 at the time. This was before we were making any real money, but we could have been making 10 times more and I don't think it would have made a difference. It was embarrassing to be getting a lecture from the hotel manager for something so stupid, costly and avoidable. But it was doubly embarrassing when the manager had obviously spoken to Gene Simmons first, because I saw Gene in the distance rolling his eyes.

I'm sure it's a rite of passage for every band to trash a room on their first tour. Some even make a habit out of it because it's part of their image. Take for example Mötley Crüe. They're constantly looking for new ways to shock everybody because they're Motley… and Motley's image IS to be excessive and shocking. But experienced pros like Gene and Kiss don't have the tolerance to suffer stupid, costly and embarrassing rites of passage. And when I saw Gene Simmons rolling his eyes, I realized Gene was taking this personally because we were his band's opening act and the hotel considered us part of his entourage.

Gene had too much class to rant or make scene. He just took me aside and told me to book separate hotels for Bonjovi for the rest

One of David's post-show rituals

of the tour. Fun is fun, but business is business, and there's so much that can go wrong on the road that you don't take the chance of repeating the same mistake twice. Lesson learned for the band. And even though I didn't have a hand in trashing the room, it was a good lesson learned for me too. NEVER let the same mistake happen twice. I was fortunate enough to learn that from "the best", and to learn it early.

Just as I never knew anyone in Bon Jovi to take the stage under the influence of recreational drugs, the same was true for Kiss. Like Jon, Kiss was all-business, all the time. That's not to say recreational drugs and women weren't everywhere. They were. But most of the time

All-business, all of the time

they came in through the crew, guests or business associates and were there for the benefit of just about everyone but the band. At least that was the case with Bon Jovi.

Drugs and women also get on tours through the business relationships. For example, let's say we use a certain brand name guitar, drums, amplifier or microphone. Well, that's part of a paid business relationship and endorsement which has value to the band in that it gets equipment for free or at a nominal cost. And it has value for the supplier, who is leveraging the relationship in their advertising, hoping that every new musician who likes Bon Jovi buys an "X" Brand guitar for example. Well, to cement that relationship, the rep from "X" Guitars will visit the band on the road and girls with him. And those girls will be very friendly and very discreet. Those same guys may also bring recreational drugs or something else you might want or need in order to 'bond' with you. I'm not saying that that is ALWAYS the case. But do you see how that can work? It's the same as in ANY business.

Once the show starts, everyone's partying except the band and crew who are actually 100% hard-at-work, trying to put on the best show they can. Make no mistake, the amazing feeling that you get at a Bon Jovi or Kiss show that you're at the party of a lifetime is a carefully contrived illusion crafted by people who are actually working their asses off. It's real alright. But it is, after all, show business. And every moment of your experience is refined and perfected over the course of hundreds of performances to make you feel like you are singularly in the best place to be on the face of the earth. And only when you understand that it is

Jon and Richie S with Ovation Guitars'
rep Rick Whelden and two lady friends

Jon in an F-16 cockpit at the 86th Tactical Fighter Wing in Ramstein AFB

a business do you really appreciate how amazing a feat that really is. You could look at any business, in any industry, on any continent on the face of the earth, and you'd be hard-pressed to find harder working people than in American and European rock and roll. That's one of the reasons it's always exported well all over the world. Youth connects to its passion regardless of culture, country, customs or language.

That show-time work ethic spilled over into just about everything we did. Jon and I were such goody-two shoes that neither of us wanted our girlfriends to smoke— they actually had to sneak away like high-schoolers if they wanted to smoke a cigarette. And when I caught them on one occasion, they BOTH made me swear not to tell Jon. There's

Patti and Dorothea sneak a cigarette

a natural tendency for stars to become tyrannical. The people around them want to please and not disappoint. It's all very well-intended, but it leads to people keeping most of their real thoughts, opinions and feelings to themselves, and depriving the star of the honest feedback he needs to keep both feet on the ground. They do more and more to try and please him until he is SO used to having things done for him that no one can possibly live up to his expectations. Eventually, everyone disappoints him. You can see how it happens, and how it's really not the star's fault.

I was really looking forward to the end of the tour on November 5th.

None of us had a lot of accounting training, and Europe really threw us a curveball because this was 1984…11 years before the Euro became the common currency for Europe.

So each of the eight countries we just toured had its own currency and the crew's production manager, Gordy Paul, had no idea how to convert everything back to dollars to reconcile his books.

Before the first time I left for Europe, Jay Sendick from our accounting office showed me how to do International accounting, and I was meticulous about it. But Gordy didn't know what he was doing, and I was afraid he'd get fired for screwing it up.

I couldn't hold it against him. Gordy started off the tour without any gear because every bit of it was accidentally misrouted to Helsinki when we we're actually starting the tour in France! So when he ended up getting behind in his bookkeeping at the end of the tour, I knew it wasn't because he had been slacking off. Gordy had been busy trying to replace virtually every piece of equipment at considerable cost with considerable time and effort—and at this point, I needed to step up and cover for him. In fact, we never did get our equipment back for that leg of the European tour until we had returned to the states and the tour was over.

The Cayman Islands vacation at the end of the "Runaway" tour started off great

So instead of going to the party, I went back to my hotel room and worked through the night trying to reconstruct and reconcile the crew budget for Gordy. Richie and David popped in a few times to ask me when I was coming to the Kiss party, but I ended up going through the night cranking the numbers. As it would turn out, I would miss my opportunity to attend the Kiss and Bon Jovi after-party, but David and Richie intended to get me blind, crippled, and crazy once we got back and headed down to the Cayman Islands with the band after the tour!

As the "Runaway" tour wound down, a lavishly insane end-of-tour party and a week to chill out awaited us down in the Caymans. The end-of-tour parties in the Caymans were with the band, girlfriends, close business associates and family.

After a year and a half of bus touring it was a time for recreational partying and relaxation, and it wouldn't be unusual to have 10-20 business associates plus guests at an after-tour party that would go on for days. Imagine working for months in a row and then not having to do anything. No interviews. No shows. No managing backstage meets and greets. Nothing but pure rest and relaxation.

We're talking about a party lasting two weeks. Doc's associate, Glen French*, had a mansion, condos and yacht. Anything we wanted. Everybody came down with their wives or girlfriends and got a condo to stay in as their individual home base. We would go from the mansion to the yacht, to the bars, to the restaurants, and back—non-stop.

Tico and I were out with the band and crew on the yacht anchored offshore when we decided to jump in and have a swimming race to the shore. After swimming for 15 minutes I turned to Tico and said, "Tico, we're out in the middle of the fucking ocean, you crazy fucking bastard!" And as we turned around to head back, we could see the yacht had already taken off in the other direction.

Tico turned back to me to say, "You know, I think we're too far out to make it…" but we had no choice. We dug in and just kept going—taking short breaks every 10 minutes or so until we got in. I remember how thrilled I was to be able to touch the bottom. It was a relief looking at each other knowing we'd be OK, after having spent the better part of the past half-hour staring

Tico and I jumped off to swim ashore—Patti was always taking pictures

*pseudonym to protect identity

up death's asshole. I honestly don't think we would have made it were it not for the fact that the tour had really built up our endurance.

When we got back, we headed to the pier where there was a bar and a lot of commotion going on. Exhausted, we walked over to see what was going on. Turned out there was a shark hunt going on in the waters we were just swimming in, and I'm thinking I was so

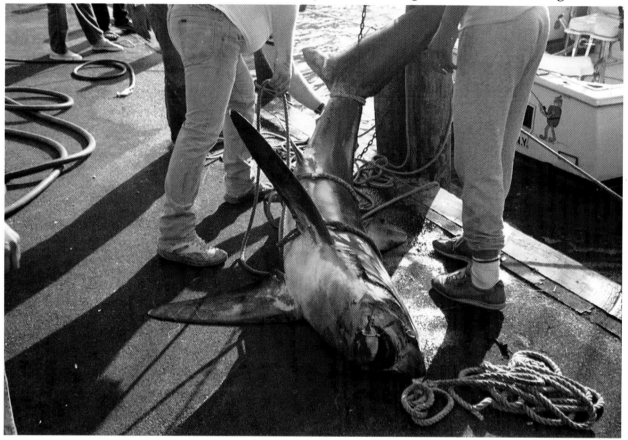

Magnificent creatures my ass—sharks will eat you and your dog so I don't mind seeing one bloodied and dead

worried about drowning that I hadn't thought about anything else. We just dodged a bullet out there, Tico. But it didn't faze Tico a bit. Sucker didn't give a shit about sharks. As for me, I didn't go back in the water for the rest of the trip.

We went from there to meet up with everybody else in the band after dinner at a local club. In addition to our families, there were two additional girls who we didn't know who came in from NY bringing coke with them. So everybody was partying and running off to the bathroom, and Richie Sambora and I suddenly became aware of the fact that we were being watched. Not by the girls or by star struck locals, but in the sense that we were under surveillance. Richie and I were starting to get a little paranoid, so I went to Jon and told him that I thought we ought to get out of there and head back to NY in the morning. We'd already been there two weeks, and I felt it was time to head back. Despite the fact that Jon never traveled without me, he insisted on staying there a few days longer even if I was going back right away. So Richie

Richie felt like we were being watched... and he was right

and I decided to leave, and we ended up on the same plane as two of the girls we didn't know who showed up at the club with coke. Jon and Dorothea stayed. As the plane was charging down the runway and about ready to lift off, the pilot suddenly cut the engines, hit the brakes and the aircraft came to a screeching halt.

He advised us we were heading back to the terminal for a maintenance issue. Richie and I cast a knowing glance at each other as we taxied back.

No sooner did the plane return to the terminal, but the door opened and two DEA officials in vests came onboard and immediately gestured to Richie and I AND the two girls seated further back, to grab our carry-ons and disembark.

Down on the tarmac, they opened up the cargo hold and instructed us to pick out our bags. This wasn't something that was new to us. Rock bands are always the target of special searches when they travel, and we were no exception. Although the girls behind us probably had just a couple of carry-on bags, Richie and I were just returning from a world tour and had 10 or 15 checked bags between us, so this was more than a little inconvenient.

But we really weren't carrying anything. The people who carry the drugs on rock tours are the business associates, crew or drivers. What I was concerned about was missing the flight and being stuck down there—or worse, having the DEA plant drugs on us. If they know the guy you work for is trafficking drugs, they're not above planting them on you to get you to give him up. And I had been with Doc long enough to know more than anyone else working for him.

As I began handing our bags down, I was telling these guys, "Look, I don't know what you're looking for, but we don't have anything," and it was true. You could be the world's

Richie Fisher planned on getting into the pot business if it was legalized

neediest user of pot, cocaine and heroine, but if you're a rock star you sure wouldn't take the chance of carrying it with you.

They pulled all our bags off the plane and began going through them and told us they already busted the two girls for cocaine—but I explained we weren't part of their entourage. After they examined two or three of our bags, I convinced the official they were wasting their time looking for contraband that we didn't have. He put the search to an end and instructed that the bags be put back onboard, then turned to us with a glare in his eye and told us to get the hell back on the plane and to never come back. They thought they knew more than they could prove.

Richie and I returned to our seats, but I knew I wasn't going to feel comfortable until we got back to Miami and I got my feet back on the ground. As the plane actually lifted off, I pushed my seat back and began to nod off. During the flight back, I flashed back to the last time I was so tormented about having drugs on a plane…

Four years earlier, I was living on the concourse in Brightwaters doing whatever entre-preneurial work came along, but without a steady gig. At the time I was living with my childhood friend Richie Fisher, who would later become Mötley Crüe's tour manager. Richie and I were both jocks—Richie was a big local football star, I was an all-state soccer player. Richie was 2 years older and shucking clams at the Oak Beach Inn on Long Island where he met a bartender named Byrdski*, and T* and Gary* who owned a restaurant called the Golden Leaf in Bay Shore. Richie, Byrdski and I were having lunch at the Golden Leaf when I looked over at T sitting in silence at the bar, reading a newspaper article. It was about how Castro opened the doors of his prisons and flooded South Florida with nearly 3000 Cuban criminals via the Mariel Boatlift, creating a free-for-all in drug trafficking that the INS and Coast Guard didn't have the manpower to control. It was the real-life setting for the movie Scarface in which hundreds of people scrambled to get into the drug business all at once and there wasn't enough law-enforcement to go around. It was T who came over to the table and brought Gary with him to tell us an idea he had for a new business. The business would

*pseudonyms to protect identity

become one of the biggest pot smuggling operations of its time, based on the supposition that without sufficient law enforcement, priorities were going to focus on hard drugs, and the lack of sufficient resources might well result in the legalization of pot in the near future. T was a true entrepreneur, a visionary who perceived the opportunity similar to the way many bootleggers saw the beer,

42 EAST MAIN STREET, BAY SHORE, NEW YORK 11706
516-███-9866

wine and liquor business near the end of prohibition, and he wanted to be in there at the ground floor.

In addition to being a bartender, Byrdski was also a skilled pilot. Together with contacts they had on the distribution side, the plan was simple—they would bring pot up from Columbia to south Florida via plane, then to the Northeast via a camper, and right to the Golden Leaf, where they could distribute inconspicuously through the restaurant. When pot was legalized, they'd already have their supply chain in place and ready to scale up.

Byrdski with his Piper Twin Comanche before our ill-fated Columbian run

They had the whole thing rolling inside of a month. Gary and T were the principals who bankrolled everything. Byrdski and Richie were the air transportation, and some hired help drove the camper.

Richie Fisher would fly with Byrdski to help him load and unload cargo—sometimes as much as a half-ton at a time—and fly it to South Florida where they would rendezvous with a camper along a desolate stretch of road called Alligator Alley in the middle of the night. From the air, they could see 50 miles in each direction, put the plane down, unload and reload it all into the camper before a single car came along. Then the camper would head back north inconspicuously through the tourist areas of Florida and up the east coast on Interstate 95, eventually to the Golden Leaf.

They had been making the trip down to Columbia every month for three months when Richie Fisher got a call from Art Voyeisk* to go on the road with the Rock group Parliament Funkadelic. At the time, Art was the sound engineer for the band and he would later come to work at McGhee Entertainment. Richie ended up taking the job and would later become tour manager for Pat Travers and hire me as Pat Travers' valet/assistant tour manager before he eventually became tour manager for Mötley Crüe. But for now, he was just going to give the job a try and make sure it was steady legitimate work before giving up his other gig. So he asked me to fill in for him for one trip. Richie Fisher was my oldest and most trusted friend, so without hesitation, I said, "Sure."

Two days later I met up with Byrdski at the Golden Leaf for a late breakfast to talk about what I was expected to do filling in for Richie. Byrdski started the discussion by reassuring me that there was nothing to worry about. He explained that when you're doing regular business together, it's not like in the movies where everybody shows up with automatic weapons and someone tries to rip off the money and the drugs. Everybody knows who everybody else is. You throw out a couple duffle bags, and you load up your cargo and you turn around and leave. It's in no one's interest to fuck anything up. No one says much and everyone does exactly what they're supposed to do as quickly as possible. Make any mistakes and you don't get shot, you just don't work anymore. This operation would eventually grow to become the second-largest pot-importing operation in the northeast because these guys knew what they were doing. Despite that and despite the popular belief that pot was going to be legalized, I wouldn't have gotten involved if it weren't for Richie needing someone to cover for him.

We left early Sunday morning, expecting to get back to Florida during the middle of the night, and home Monday morning. Only it turned into something a little more like "Gilligan's Island."

The first leg of the trip down to Florida was like a weekend outing. We were both in a slightly buzzed state, just taking in the view from the relatively lower altitude flown by

*pseudonym to protect identity

smaller planes like Byrdski's. We refueled in Miami, then headed down to Columbia—again, just taking in the view. As we got into Columbian airspace, Byrdski told me it would be all business for the next couple hours as he got on the radio with his contact on the ground. The ride got turbulent as we flew over Boyoca and into the mountains. We were in the clouds—what seemed like miles up in the sky—when suddenly the clouds broke and I could see we were just a couple hundred feet above the ground. In the heavy overcast, we landed in a plowed field lit by burning gasoline canisters.

When we opened the doors, I saw the bales being brought over to us on several flatbed hand trucks while a pickup truck loaded with five gallon containers of gas was already parked next to the plane. Four guys with holstered handguns, sunglasses and fatigues stood with their hands on their hips waiting for the hand trucks to be brought up. Jay threw out three bags of cash and told me to wait as they gave them a quick check. Then he gestured toward the pickup and I got out and started pulling out the 5-gallon cans and fueling up.

It took every bit of an hour to fuel-up and my arms were already tired before I started loading the bales. Then we were given the go-ahead to begin loading the 2 foot by 3 foot bales. Just as we were about to load the last two bales, another Columbian carrying an assault rifle stepped up and said, "No...THESE," gesturing to two large duffle bags. Byrdski tried to correct him and no sooner did he get a syllable out of his mouth, when the guy walked right up to my face, and with the gun right between my eyes, pulled the lever back to cock it and said, "THESE." So I raised my hands and slowly and got out to pick up the two duffle bags, and then I got back in—leaving the two bales of pot on one of the flatbed hand trucks. Then the gunman stepped up to the plane and boarded, sitting directly behind me with the gun to my head. He handed Byrdski a card with GPS coordinates in it for Miraflores, Panama and told us to go. We weren't sure if we'd been hijacked or whether our payload had been. At that point it just seemed pretty certain we were going to get killed and the pot was going to be ripped off. But nobody explained anything.

No one makes jokes under those circumstances, except Byrdski who either had a death wish or a remarkably astute grasp of what was going on around him. He kept taunting the guy with the gun to see how far he could go. He acted like he didn't speak English OR Spanish and spoke in some kind of broken Italian. He'd stop talking every few seconds and offer the guy with the gun the wheel as if to say, "Here, you drive..." I mean, the balls on this guy.

I don't remember much about the flight except that it seemed like an eternity. The only words spoken during a particularly bumpy segment of the nearly two hour trip were when the guy with the gun pressed the barrel against the back of Byrdski's head and gently pushed it forward to punctuate the words "no turbulence." Meanwhile, Byrdski was humming Bert Bacharach tunes like nothing was going on.

We were directed to land just shy of the mountains in Miraflores, Panama on another plowed runway. All kinds of thoughts went through my head as the plane came in for a landing. What was this guy going to do to us now that he got the ride he wanted? Was he going to shoot us, steal the cargo, or both? As the plane came to a rest I remember waiting to hear the trigger. But instead, our stowaway just pushed me aside and opened the door and jumped out without saying a word. Then he directed me to throw out the two duffle bags of cocaine—and I did. And then, he just said dismissively, "GO," and that's all we had to hear. At that point, we were just overjoyed to be alive. But we had given them all the money and we were two bales short on the count. PLUS, now that we made this detour to Panama, we didn't have enough fuel to get to the rendezvous point and no place to safely refuel with our cargo on-board, so we knew things were about to get worse.

As we headed back toward South Florida, we found out how much worse. We were definitely 20 or 30 gallons shy on fuel. We kept making our way north on instruments, but looking for places we could land and perhaps fuel up. Byrdski headed toward Turks and Caicos, knowing there were a number of uncharted islands up that way. Assuming we found a place to refuel, we would have to take the chance of landing there or risk going down in the shark-infested ocean.

Just before dusk, we spotted a small island about 680 miles east-southeast of Miami, and Byrdski began circling it while we still had gas—doing reconnaissance on what was down there and figuring out the best place to land. It was getting dark but still clear with a nearly full moon when the engine began to sputter and we ran out of gas. As the plane lost power, the eerie sound of wind blowing against the fuselage filled the void left by the suddenly silent engines.

As we began to descend, Byrdski glanced from side to side at the moonlit landscape looking for 50 yards of clearing to put down the plane safely. We glided in at about 50 miles an hour and crashed as the sand suddenly got a hold of our right landing gear, thrusting the forward part of the right wing downward into the sand where the beach trailed off into the ocean. The crash had severely damaged the right landing gear and bent the right prop, leaving the aircraft unable to take off or fly—even if we had fuel to do it. But we were safe and, for a faint moment, overjoyed for the second time that day just to be alive!

When it dawned on us that we would have a shitload of explaining to do if we lost a couple hundred thousand dollars worth of pot AND the plane, we immediately started looking for a place to stash the pot in case we had been spotted. We didn't want to use the radio to call for help for fear of not knowing who was going to show up. We had to hide our cargo and reach out to our own guys before anyone else found us or found our payload.

It's funny that you just start running on instinct when things get out of control. Sore and a bit bruised, we carried our payload bale by bale, hundreds of feet away from the plane to the higher ground inland. We took turns digging an 8' x 8' x 5' hole with a folding hand shovel and carrying up bales. After about 14 hours of digging, dragging and burying bales, all the cargo was out of the plane and nearly completely buried 400 feet from the crash site. By about 6 PM, Monday we had finished and we literally passed-out at the plane for at least 5 hours. We woke up tired and thirsty and made our way down to the only huts on the island, which were populated by fishermen. We were met outside by Garnu, a 60-or-70-something year-old Topanga fisherman, slight yet muscular, with dark, leathery skin. We told him our plane ran out of gas and we needed a phone. He explained there were no phones anywhere on the island, but agreed to take us to Salt Cay, some 30 miles away, where there were more people and at least one phone that he knew of.

Garnu lived on a diet of fresh fish and canned vegetables. He took us in and made Snapper and canned green beans for dinner. The next morning, he ferried us over to Salt Cay. It was about noon on Tuesday by the time Byrdski was able to get through to Gary and T and tell them what happened. The camper had waited for us until Monday before heading back up north, and they had all been wondering where we were. After Byrdski finished talking with T, he spent another hour talking to Gary, giving him a full account of what was wrong with the plane. It would take at least three or four days for them to fly down to Miami and get a boat and materials to come out after us. In the meantime, we would stay with Garnu and help him ferry his cargo out to Salt Cay on days he wasn't fishing.

By Friday morning, Gary and T arrived by boat with parts, a mechanic for the plane, sleeping bags, water, eight 5-gallon cans of fuel, some cold cuts and water in a cooler, and a couple of freelancers from the Golden Leaf for additional manpower. By Friday afternoon we had everything at the site and work began on the plane. Gary started a fire and opened the cooler full of cold cuts, water and a case of clams and Miller Lite, and so for the first time in a few days, I actually started to relax. We doused the fire at dusk, slept out and finished the

Our rescue boat and 2 zodiacs seen from Byrdski's plane

landing gear repair late Saturday morning. Gary pointed out that the place where we put the pot was hidden from traffic on the ground, but out in the open and probably easily visible from the air. So we moved it all once more while the repairs were being made, put a tarp over it and attempted to camouflage it with bushes, branches and fronds.

The mechanic and the new help kept going back to the boat for tools because we were constantly running into problems trying to switch out old and rusted parts on the plane. With each passing minute we all started feeling increasingly concerned about getting out of there before anyone spotted us or reported what was going on—the biggest concern being pirates.

By early Sunday, the prop had finally been replaced and landing gear repaired, and Byrdski fired it up to make sure everything was working. I decided I had tempted fate one too many times on this trip and asked Gary and T if I could go back with them instead of flying, and they were fine with that. One of the new guys would accompany Byrdski

Gary and T relax after plane is repaired...
bales of pot fill entire rear of fuselage

and I would take the boat to Turks and Caicos and fly back from there. We spent the next 5 hours loading up the plane and by 3 PM we were done. But everyone hung out until Byrdski took off just before dusk to rendezvous with the camper on Alligator Alley, exactly one week late.

On the boat trip back, Gary confided in me that he would have preferred to have picked up the payload with another plane, and just burned the other one and put in an insurance claim on it—rather than having spent so much time exposed out here. Gary was probably right, though it was always more important to T for everyone to be on the same page than "right."

After a trip like that you have to ask yourself whether any good came out of it, and I would definitely say "yes." You see, it was that specific experience that led me to look for a job where I was in control and had both feet on the ground... which is why I took a job driving a limo. And that's how I would eventually become Doc McGhee's driver and be offered the job as Bon Jovi's tour manager. But I thought the limo business was also good for me because I was too high-strung to be anywhere near drug trafficking.

But as I woke up on the airliner with Richie, heading back to the U.S. after our vacation in the Cayman Islands, and I reflected on how the officials at the airport in the Caymans treated us, I became alarmed that perhaps I hadn't gotten as far away from drug smugglers and the drug smuggling business as I thought— in fact, as it would turn out, my move to the limo company and my subsequent move to McGhee would actually get me progressively more involved in it!

After Richie Sambora and I touched down in Miami and we cleared customs, we were ecstatic... No, we didn't have anything on us or in our bags, but we were

Richie and I were ecstatic to be back in the U.S.

convinced these guys were so determined to bust us for cocaine that they would have had no qualms about planting it on us to do it. I was just happy to have safely landed! I called Jon as soon as we checked into the hotel in Miami, and he asked us to wait for him in Miami because he was going to change his plans and get the hell out of there the next morning. When Jon and Dorothea arrived at the airport, they were both strip-searched (complete with anal cavity searches) before they were allowed to embark. We later found out that the night before, the U.S. government dispatched Navy Seals to come ashore in the middle of the night to kidnap Doc's friend and business partner Glen French from the compound (while we were staying there) in order to extradite him to the U.S. But somehow, by chance or by design, he had eluded capture. He was Doc McGhee's best friend and business associate, and as we later learned, one of the biggest cocaine smugglers in the United States. And law enforcement obviously thought we were in it with him, rather than just being his guests. He would continue to evade capture until nearly a year later, when he boarded a plane bound for Mexico City with (Tommy Lee and Heather Locklear) and the FAA diverted the flight to New York's JFK, where the DEA and FBI were waiting for him and took him into custody!

Producer Lance Quinn and sound engineer Obie O'Brien craft the band's raw, powerhouse sound

When I got back home, I was shaken, but full of optimism. The band was going back to the studio to record its second album. Patti and I were about to get engaged. And my plan was to recharge my batteries for a couple months, go back on tour, put a few more years into Bon Jovi on the road, earn the stake that Doc promised when I first came on board, and ultimately get married and retire from the road—continuing to work with the band out of the main office

Tico and Jon arrive at the Warehouse on the first day of recording 7800 Degrees Fahrenheit

on Central Park South. There wasn't much time between the end of the "Runaway" Tour and the beginning of the "7800" Tour. The former ended in December of '84, and the latter was to start in March '85. That left barely 3 months to get the second album completed.

Polygram sent the band back to the Warehouse in Philadelphia where most of the songs from the first album were recorded. I was working out of McGhee Entertainment's NY office at 240 Central Park South in NYC while we were off the road. The band took a small apartment just around the corner from the studio.

Everyone popped in from time to time. Jon's dad John came around every Monday with a pot of homemade sauce and everyone had spaghetti. All week. Every week.

The objective of the 2nd album was to appeal to older girls and deliver a higher percentage of males to the franchise with a heavier, more masculine rock sound. It was decided to christen the second album "7800 Degrees Fahrenheit" to celebrate the raw powerhouse sound crafted by producer Lance Quinn and sound engineer Obie O'Brian because that's the temperature at which rock actually melts down and liquefies into lava. Everything looked like it was on track. But things were about to take a frightening turn.

ONE STEP FORWARD, TWO STEPS BACK

On March 26th, 1985, the day after I left NY to go out on the "7800° Fahrenheit" tour, the Suffolk County District Attorney and DEA showed up at my brother's house in West Islip to arrest me for cocaine trafficking! Just days earlier, my old boss at the limo company, Harry Feingold, was busted for being the mastermind of a huge cocaine smuggling operation—the biggest ever of its time—and the DEA produced a transcript of a wiretapped conversation between me and Harry which they said proved I was a part of the operation!

I couldn't believe what I was hearing. In reality, Harry had called McGhee Entertainment back in January, just before we headed off to Philadelphia to record the new album, to speak with Doc or someone else in the office, and I answered the phone. I knew Harry because he owned the limo company I used to work for, and we shared a little small talk. At the time, I made some comment to him about "snow coming" and "10 degree temperatures," and some rocket scientist at DEA interpreted the word "snow" as meaning "cocaine" and "10 degrees" as "ten ounces." And if you think nobody is that stupid, here are copies of the actual wiretapped transcript and their interpretation of it that they used to try to indict me.

Actual Wiretapped Transcript:

R=RICHIE (JOHN DOE 1, a/k/a RICH)
H-HARRY FEINGOLD

H   Hello

R   H, what's going on buddy

H   Hey, buddy

R   How you doing today, alright

H   Good man, good

R   Looks like we may get snowed in tomorrow, you never know

H   Yeah

R   I hope not, now let me ask you H, what time am I going to see you

H   Well, I'll, I, let me give you a call, let me give you tomorrow, let me give you a call tomorrow

R   Yeah, because, ah

H   Ah (inaudible) I have a lot of running around to do and if it's really snowy out, (inaudible) I don't, I don't know what's going on

R   Well, do me a favor, also man, give me a call before you do anything because, it's going to be like you know one zero

H   It's really snowy out, going to be 10 degrees out, huh

R   Yeah exactly man, it's tough, okay, so just give me a call tomorrow H

H   Alright Buddy

R   Bye, bye

747-8600

The actual conversation is merely a little small talk between Harry and me. But the following is the DEA interpretation of that conversation.

DEA Interpretation:

a/k/a RICH says, "well, do me a favor, also man, give me a call before you do anything because it's going to be like you know one zero", JOHN DOE 1, a/k/a RICH is ordering ten ounces of cocaine from HARRY FEINGOLD. HARRY FEINGOLD tries to disguise this phrase by referring to ten degrees. The two end the conversation by agreeing to talk tomorrow.

32. Pursuant to the aforementioned amended eavesdropping order on telephone instrument number (516) 669-90██, a call was intercepted on February 6, 1985, at approximately 4:59 p.m. in which HARRY FEINGOLD, using telephone instrument number (516) 669-90██, calls out to telephone instrument number (212) ███-7300 and speaks with a female identified as JULIE who puts JOHN DOE 1, a/k/a RICH on the phone. The following is a true and accurate transcript of that conversation:

Again, the DEA interpreted the word "snow" to mean "cocaine" and the words "10 degrees" to mean "ten ounces." And on that basis, they wanted to indict me for cocaine trafficking!

Granted, I knew Harry was in the coke smuggling business. At a family party around Christmas '83, I told my cousin, a New York City narcotics officer, that I was working for a limo company on the island and he responded, "Not Sophisticated Gents? That's a front for a million-dollar a week cocaine smuggling operation, and they use the limos to shuttle deliveries and pick up cash...you get your ass out of there..." At the time, I knew Harry was smuggling cocaine and Doc was smuggling pot, and that both of them had business together, so I gave Harry a "heads-up" and shortly afterwards stopped driving limos for Harry because Doc asked me to be the valet/assistant tour manager for Pat Travers.

Now it seemed the DEA was trying to set me up on a trumped up charge--either to get me to implicate everybody, or because they really thought I HAD to be in on it because I was so close to Doc and Harry. Once I found out Harry was in the cocaine business, I got out of there before getting mixed up in it. But I was now beginning to understand how extensive Harry's operation was—in fact the most extensive ever uncovered in the county—so I shouldn't have been surprised to see how many people I knew were involved in it.

Rather than turn myself in for something I had no part in, I went to the library and looked up weather reports for NYC to prove that when I was talking with Harry it really was about the weather. Then I gave my lawyer this copy of the N.Y. Times weather report in NYC the day of the wiretapped conversation proving that snow and 10 degree temperatures were actually forecast.

Actual weather forecast presented by my lawyer to the DEA

But even my lawyer didn't believe me—he just told me to turn myself in. But I couldn't. I was innocent and now going out on my second world tour with Bon Jovi, and I wanted to stick with it because Doc had the cash to put them on the road and keep them on the road until we had the whole act running on all cylinders, and I wanted to really see this through. Plus, Doc had promised me 5% of the band and I was determined to break the band to make that percentage mean something.

But what a price to pay. It was hard enough to do the job of tour manager, but now, every day we were on tour, I expected the FBI or DEA to come storming in to take me away in handcuffs. Every time anything noisy or surprising happened I thought it was the feds busting in to haul me away. Every time we crossed the border going into another country,

I expected the customs officials to have my name, pick me up and extradite me. And every time we went through a travel checkpoint I worried that some hotshot DEA prick who "knew" I was guilty would plant drugs in my bags in order to charge me with smuggling and bring me in.

As I played back in my mind all the events of the recent past, I began to speculate how Doc could have used me to move drugs and money for him on numerous occasions.

For example, right after Mötley was signed, Doc asked me to drive the beat-up, 6-year old Impala you see below from Miami to Mötley Crüe tour manager Richie Fisher out in Marina Del Rey, California, so the band would have transportation in California. But that didn't

This is the Impala Doc asked me to drive to California and deliver to Mötley Crüe tour manager

make sense. Nicer, less beat-up cars could be bought in California for a cheaper price. And why would he select a low-end, middle-American car for a band that signed with Doc because he treated them like rock stars, if the whole idea wasn't to just cross the country to deliver something in the car and not draw attention to the car along the way? Mötley never did use the car and never complained about it; I was pretty sure the car was loaded with cash or cocaine when I drove it out there.

On yet another occasion, Doc had me tow a 21' lake boat from Miami to International Falls, Minnesota with a two-day layover in

his hometown of Chicago. No one would ever bring a 21' boat 1500 miles to International Falls because the place is loaded with them and they can be bought or rented for next to nothing. The only reason to tow one there that I can think of would be to bring something else in the boat or trailer. I was aware that Doc was distributing pot and coke as far west as Chicago at the time, and fifteen minutes after I arrived there, they were all snorting coke on Doc's houseboat.

And still another time I was asked to bring back to the U.S. an 8' marlin that Doc had supposedly caught in the Cayman Islands. This was an "emergency" trip to the Caymans,

Mötley at US Festival—no one in the band or management ever used the car

and Doc would use the word "emergency" mainly when he was out of money and needed cash. So Doc sent me down on his private plane with his private pilot, Rick Warner*, to get the marlin.

Once I got there, I had to wait two days for a fish that was already caught and frozen, before I could load it up and fly it back to the Ft. Lauderdale General Aviation terminal. That didn't make any sense.

I figured the only reason there would be a delay was if they had to thaw and refreeze the marlin in order to put something in it—like cash or coke. You could fit 10 kilos of coke in an 8' marlin—at that time $300K street value—or a half million in cash in large bills. The point was that no one at the General Aviation terminal at Ft. Lauderdale was going to look inside a frozen marlin to figure out what, if anything was inside. So I just chilled down there while the fish was being prepped, then flew it back when it was ready, and took it directly to the office in Miami. Two days later there was no longer any cash shortage at the office, and

I flew to the Cayman Islands to pick up a frozen 8' marlin

*pseudonym to protect identity

We didn't mind waiting in the Caymans for the marlin to be prepped

two weeks later a mounted marlin appeared on the wall (although I'm pretty sure it wasn't the one I brought back). I figured the one I brought back was emptied out and the fish was chopped up. Haven't had tuna fish since then.

Anytime I was asked to do something—by Doc or by Jon—I saw it as an opportunity for me to prove how trustworthy and reliable I was. I wanted to be perceived as the "go-to" guy, and "go-to" guys get it done—and ask 'why' later. At the time I often turned a blind eye to what was going on, or didn't think about it at all. But now I was banking on making a career with Bon Jovi and I couldn't take the chance of losing it. Once I understood that I had been working for three huge drug operations—Doc's, Doc's friend Harry and Doc's friend Glen in the Caymans—and that they were all under surveillance and even my personal phone calls

I had a growing concern that I could be set up as a "fall guy"

were being tapped, I knew I had to be careful to avoid creating even the appearance of being involved in smuggling or distribution.

I had become privy to everything, but I couldn't quit—because I had been promised an ownership stake in the band, and I would have to stick around to get it. Moreover, I wanted this job. I was good at it, and the band members were like my brothers. I had my share of pot and cocaine and I enjoyed using it. But I didn't want anything to do with smuggling or distributing it. My only hope was that Bon Jovi would become a successful and self-funding headlining act faster than Doc, Harry or Glen's drug operations would collapse—and take me down with them.

THE 7800° FAHRENHEIT TOUR

In April and May of 1985, Bon Jovi headlined 3,000 seat venues in Europe and Japan. In May, the band began a 6-month run of U.S. tour dates supporting Ratt (in the midst of that tour, we managed to make appearances at Castle Donington in England, and at the very first Farm Aid). As we started the tour, Jon and I were relentless in cultivating the radio and record company reps, and that eventually paid off because when we came back to these towns the second time around, these radio stations, publishing contacts, and label reps were 100% responsive and supportive because Jon had made them his friends the first time around. If nothing else, we were building the fan base by getting more airplay.

Jon and the band receive a hero's welcome at Nagaya train station in Japan

Jon always wanted to give the fans the highest energy show, but it was hard to keep pace with the demands of touring, doing all the publicity, and being the front man. So Alec used to cut Jon a piece of speed to take with a Jolt cola before each show. It was Jon's way of trying to give the audience the best show he could. As time went on, he also needed to drink more wine to relax after the show, and more Valium or Halcion to go to sleep so that he could do it all over again with a new live audience the next day. This routine kicked in at full force around the time the band began to headline because the stage got bigger and took more energy to cover.

Acknowledgment Sent

--More--

Paul:
I Have a bill for $600 for shipping
Jolt cola to Australia. Please advise.
... show on Sept. 25, please
... 3 down for ... the

Jolt Cola with speed was Jon's beverage of choice before going on stage

By this point, even though Jon was doing everything humanly possible to take care of his voice, Doc had the band on such a rigorous schedule that it left Jon's vocal chords raw, swollen and bleeding. So I would take Jon into the city to get prednisone prescriptions from Dr. Kessler, or have doctors come in to give him corticosteroid injections while we were on the road. Jon would do just about anything to keep from disappointing the fans.

Bon Jovi's amazing energy level on stage has driven its appeal for the past 25 years

At some point you realize that the audience is only operating on this level for one night and that you're actually playing to a new live audience every single day, but it doesn't matter when the first thing on your mind is giving your audience a show that beats their expectations. When you think about it, it's impossible to keep pace with the demands of a continuously re-energized audience. But Bon Jovi did it, and that's what I think the fans have always recognized—Jon and the band's super-human commitment to the fans. It's more addictive than any drug because it's plugged directly into your desire to be a star and make your audience happy. You crave it and can't stop trying to give back to the audience more than you get. It can drive you to the edge and take you to recreational or addictive use. Everyone, including myself, enjoyed using some drugs recreationally. But not Jon. He did what he had to do to do a show, and that was it. But that didn't matter. He was a target for the DEA and law enforcement at every turn. And I was, too.

Superlative execution and unbridled passion drive Richie's live performance

Just as the tour was getting underway we were in the middle of shooting the "Only Lonely" video at the Seaside Park boardwalk. Principal photography was done during the day but Director Martin Kahan had the shoot going throughout the night with different call times for each member of the band's pickup shots. When Jon was wrapped, he and I headed back to the hotel. At about 5 AM I got a call that the director was arrested for cocaine and was hauled off to jail. Great! I'm already under surveillance for suspected cocaine trafficking and Jon doesn't use cocaine, yet everybody else is parading around using it with impunity. Thankfully, they had the sense to not use the shit while Jon and I were on the set. That's why we had to be emphatic about drug use: because if anything came down while we were there, the star could end up out of commission and I could end up in jail for the duration.

When we were flying to the UK in a commercial airliner, Alec, David and Richie kept heading off to the bathroom in the forward part of the plane to do freebase. Soon the actual smell of the burning pot and coke began to build up outside the bathroom and the pilot, who had stepped out of the cockpit, obviously detected the odor.

When we arrived in London, once again Jon's bags and my bags were thoroughly searched by customs officials who were obviously tipped off by the flight crew. Jon and I were totally clean, but we were held up for hours. Meanwhile, Alec, David and Richie breezed right through. Alec liked to store private things in the heel of his shoe, at a time when no one inspected shoes. But for some reason, nobody even bothered him or any of them.

We arrived in the UK totally jet-lagged and on a heavy dose of Halcion, and I had this surreal nightmare that I killed everyone in the band in their sleep. I was telling Richie the story when he told me he had the exact same nightmare, and he was doubly freaked because when he woke up he said he wasn't sure whether or not it really happened. Well, that was it for Halcion for Richie and me. Our next stop was Germany—where Valium is sold over-the-counter, without a prescription. I literally bought out the entire available inventory in every city—something like 400 30-packs of Valium—a total of nearly 12,000 freakin' pills. It was enough to fill an entire Halliburton suitcase. We were determined to never go near that Halcion shit again.

Jon had been in a strange mood, too. I'm not sure if it was because of the pills or not—he'd been arguing more and more with Dorothea, who Patti told me was growing weary of the lack of the commitment associated with the touring lifestyle. But there were other "little'" things that Dorothea was pissed off about.

At the beginning of the tour, when we were still in Japan, Patti, Dorothea and Wendy came out to visit for a couple weeks, and Patti told me about how the three of them met at the hotel and Wendy suggested they order drinks and lunch, and Dorothea jumped in and said, "Oh, no, I can't do that— Jon will have a fit!" She was concerned that Jon would go ballistic over her spending his money on food or drinks without his permission. Patti interjected that she would order and charge it to her room, and Wendy interjected that she would order and charge it to her room. Dorothea, a bit

Jon feeling worn-out and wondering if stardom was ever going to happen

embarrassed, acknowledged that that would probably be the best thing. The girls knew something was up, but they weren't sure what it was...

But what may have been the icing on the cake was when Jon came down with a case of "crabs" in Japan. It may have been from a visit to a public bath house, or too close social contact with all the fashion models constantly traveling to Japan to appear in Japanese advertising who were always scrambling to take pictures with him. Anyway, in Japan, nobody has any body hair, so they never even heard of "crabs," much less have the meds to get rid of them. Meanwhile, Jon has a coat of fur like a goddamned pony and the crabs were everywhere. I brought him to a bunch of local doctors and eventually to a hospital where they actually tried to pull them off individually with tweezers. Jon came running out in pain screaming, "Let's get out of here!!" We needed meds, and even if we got them when we arrived back to the States, Jon would still need a few days to get the symptoms under control, and that was going to be a problem.

The bottom line was Jon had to go back to the states with the crabs, and that may have had something to do with Dorothea being upset with him and the problems between them during the weeks that followed. We had a month off before going back on the road in the U.S. opening for Ratt. But as the band went back on the road in August, Dorothea was no longer calling Jon and it became obvious to me that something had happened between the two of them. Dorothea had finally had it and had broken up with Jon.

I believe it was around then Diane Lane showed up backstage for the first time for one of the band's shows in Irvine, CA in early August, and she and Jon immediately hit it off. Diane was 3 years younger than Jon, and for Jon, meeting her was like going back a few years to a less complicated time. Diane loved to party and have fun, and she had a real aptitude for the partying lifestyle. She managed to keep Jon reasonably happy through his break-up with Dorothea, a time during which I felt Jon was feeling more than a little bit vulnerable and isolated.

In the midst of the tour we managed to make an appearance at Castle Donington's "Monsters of Rock" concert in England. That's the annual day-long summer festival for heavy rock and metal bands where 100,000 of the world's most critical fans hammer you with a barrage of rocks, mud and piss in plastic bottles if you're an opening act. Bon Jovi was third to go on August 17, 1985, and the band put on a hell of a show. But hours after the show the band was still scraping mud sand and gravel out of their eyes, mouths and ears, and trying to wash the piss smell out of their noses. This concert was a defining moment because in the end, it's all about headlining, and the band's music wasn't yet at the level it needed to be in order to be headlining. The "7800° Fahrenheit" album would be the last album the band would ever record without outside songwriting help. And it was in no small part due to that August 17 show in Donington.

About a month after Donington, the band played the 1st Farm Aid on September 22, 1985.

This was a real tough show because we played the night before almost 400 miles away in La Crosse, Wisconsin. It was well after midnight when we got on the bus for Champaign,

Illinois, still wired from just having finished the show. I think we got an hour or so of sleep before pulling into town at 9 AM. Then the band had an hour to shower and get dressed for our opening spot at 11:30 AM. It was a privilege to meet music legends Neil Young and Willie Nelson, who were as gracious as could be and especially courteous and professional hosts. But we were toast by the time our set was over, and we headed right back north again to get back on the tour schedule.

Elmo asks to stop for food before bus leaves for Champaign, Illinois

The "7800° Fahrenheit" album generated lukewarm critical response, and Doc thought the answer was to toughen-up Bon Jovi's image and make them more like Mötley Crüe. From the time Doc signed Jon, Jon and the band were constantly in the shadow of Mötley Crüe because they were the big name headlining band inside McGhee Entertainment.

So on September 23rd, the day after Farm Aid, we would be in Detroit, Michigan on an off day before playing a show there on Tuesday. The idea was to hire a photographer to shoot an "after-show party" with a few scantily clad girls, and then put some pictures out on the PR newswire and a promotion in the trades, hoping to incentivize the trade papers to publish feature articles on the band that

I'm always working, so David is impressed to see me sitting down

month. They asked me to call in a favor with a photographer who would bring in some girls. While the shoot was going on, I had a meeting with a big local radio station to talk about how to get more radio play for the band.

No one had any idea what Doc wanted or what Polygram expected, or how to get it, so the guys just did what they thought would be cool. A few days later, we got a call from one of the girls at Polygram assigned to the job. She'd seen a few of the pictures and deemed them unusable for any kind of commercial use because the girls were topless. In her opinion, the pictures were pretty much worthless because none of them could ever be used or reprinted in the trade papers or the mainstream press. So the promotion was killed, and that was the last time anybody said anything about it or the shoot—until 2 years later when the photographer mysteriously died. For now, all marketing efforts would be properly focussed on getting better songs for the next album.

The "7800° Fahrenheit" tour could have ended up being the band's swan song because album sales were soft compared with the previous tour. But what the band had going for it at that point was its tight and powerful sound. Plus, Jon and I had worked very hard and done an amazing job cultivating all the radio stations along the way. In that sense, the "7800° Fahrenheit" tour "primed the pump" for the album that was to follow. And perhaps most importantly, Doc stayed behind them with his money. The tour started with the Suffolk County DA, DEA and FBI in pursuit of me and came to an end 9 months later with me spending virtually every minute of it looking over my shoulder, expecting to be arrested. Before the final show on the last day of the tour, Richie and the crew duct-taped me to a chair. After living in fear of getting arrested and imprisoned for the past 9 months, it seemed to be a truly fitting end to the "7800°" tour. Thankfully, Jon got me out. But in the meantime, Jon was starting to miss Dorothea—it had only been a couple months. But the very thing that made Jon feel so passionate toward Diane Lane in the first place ended up being the reason for their sudden, unceremonious break up in the end.

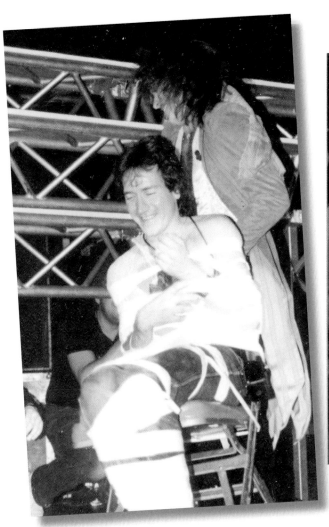

Jon helps me escape duct tape prison

Diane was young and wild and loved to party. But she loved to party so much that Jon caught her partying with Richie Sambora. That wasn't a good day for Jon's relationship with Diane, to say nothing of Jon-Richie relations.

We got back home just before Christmas 1985. The first thing I did was call Patti and I think the first thing Jon did was call Dorothea to plead with her to come back, which they did. Patti and I started looking for an apartment, and in the meantime I camped out in my office at McGhee Entertainment. It was around that time that the Mötley Crüe album went multi-platinum on their "Theatre of Pain" album and they were staying at a hotel nearby to get their awards. I gave them a half-ounce of coke, but they plowed through it by 7AM and came back to the office looking for more. Tommy woke me up screaming, "Richie, we're HIGH, where's the coke?" There was always coke at the office so I gave them another ounce and they went back to their hotel and partied all day.

I had to wake Richie Fisher up at the hotel to get him to agree to cover the cost. He just said, "Whatever it is, it's OK…" and I remember thinking how I wouldn't have been able to

Mötley shot this with real cocaine and ended up using the picture for their Christmas card

cover an expense like that with my Bon Jovi budget. At that point, Bon Jovi wasn't making money and accrued expenses amounting to millions that had to be paid back before the band saw a nickel. I remember thinking that we'd never get in the black on Bon Jovi. But I didn't anticipate the magnitude of success that was about to come. We anticipated that our total debt would take three years to repay if we were successful. But in actuality, it would be paid back in the first week of the next tour. That's how unbelievably successful "Slippery When Wet" would be.

I think the three biggest reasons the band made it were 1) Doc's money and commitment, 2) relentless touring on the part of the band, and 3) Desmond Child.

A lot of labels and managers would have given up on the band after the "7800" Album. But Doc stayed behind them with his money, and reached out to Desmond Child. And it would be BOTH those moves that would salvage the band from certain obscurity. There were dozens of people working with Doc and Derek through all those early days and through the insane stardom of "Slippery When Wet": countless radio people, tireless Polygram staffers and promoters, Derek Schulman, Ray, Julie, and Margaret at McGhee, and of course the band, crew and many more. But the transformational moment came when Desmond arrived.

Livin' On a Prayer

When we returned home after the "7800° Fahrenheit" tour, our fan base was growing and we were starting to draw an older audience as planned. Moreover, the band had gelled and the sound—which was ALWAYS good—became incredibly solid and tight. Jon's and Richie's voices were beginning to hit a startling level of near-perfection. But without Jack Ponti in the picture, Jon had not managed to write another song with the commercial appeal of "Runaway," and it was time to look to the outside for songwriting help. That's when Doc suggested bringing in Desmond Child.

Desmond knew how to write hits. He had collaborated with Paul Stanley and KISS on a total of 16 songs, including the hit "Heaven's On Fire" from the group's Animalize album in 1984. Jon loved "Heaven's On Fire," so when the idea of collaborating with Desmond was put on the table, Jon agreed—although it seemed to me he did so reluctantly.

I remember thinking how important it was for Jon to see himself as the catalyst of the band as well as its star, so when Doc brought up the idea of bringing in songwriting help, I thought there might be some push-back from Jon, but the bottom line was this: Jon wanted stardom desperately, and he knew the songs could be better. So he went along even if this particular move was somewhat humbling for him.

By this time Jon had moved into his new house in Rumson and I was spending virtually all my time there. What a pleasure it was to be able to just hang out without having to keep an eye on everything like I had to do when we were touring. When you're on tour at the end of the day you take a room next to the elevators so you can see everything coming and going to the guy's rooms. You don't go to sleep until they go to sleep. Now, suddenly, I felt like I was 10 years old again and just sleeping over at my friend's house. It was the best of times because we would talk about what we were going to do and how we were going to do it without the distractions of doing a show or being on a schedule.

View of Jon's house from the back of the yard

The day Desmond showed up at Jon's house in Rumson, Richie, a deeply spiritual person, was excited about writing a new song about a "prayer." When Desmond came over, Jon, Richie and Desmond went upstairs to the spare bedroom over the dining room and started writing while I hung out downstairs with Dorothea.

Dorothea was one of the most gracious and strong individuals I had ever met. I was close enough to Jon to know that she was, and would always be, the love of Jon's life.

Patti took this great shot of Dorothea and Jon when we all visited a temple in Kyoto

My fiancée, Patti, was close enough to Dorothea to know that she was perhaps the only person who thoroughly understood Jon, loved him with all her heart and accepted the lifestyle.

During that time, Dorothea also set me up with a chiropractor for my increasingly troublesome back. The stress of being implicated in any of Doc's or Harry's nefarious schemes was mounting up and starting to cause sharp pains in my back.

Patti became increasingly concerned that Doc could use me as a fall guy in case the ax came down on him. We didn't know what he was up to—only that every once in while he would ask me to do "favors" for him. I had stopped the "favors," but as I learned when Harry was arrested, that wouldn't necessarily keep me from being implicated. But fortunately, as we were gearing up for the "Slippery" tour, Jon asked me to spend more time out in Jersey with the band, and comparatively less time in the office, so I was starting to worry less about being in the wrong place at the wrong time.

While Jon and Richie went to work writing with Desmond, Dorothea made sandwiches and refreshments and I hung around to do whatever was needed. They weren't up there an hour before I heard the now familiar melody of "Livin' on a Prayer" for the first time— you could immediately tell it was something special. As I listened to it for the first time, it sounded so inspirational and so melodic that I had an immediate premonition it would be a big hit. Years later I heard rumors that Desmond alone wrote the song, but I knew the idea started with Richie.

Three places to sit in the unassuming spare bedroom where most of the "Slippery" hits were written

Within two weeks, two more humongous hits came out of that room with Desmond, Jon and Richie: "You Give Love a Bad Name" and "Wanted Dead or Alive."

I believe "You Give Love a Bad Name" was inspired by Jon's disappointment with Diane, and that awful feeling a guy gets when he catches someone, who has professed her undying love to only him, in a questionable situation with someone else. I think this tends to happen a lot—and most of the time, the guy doesn't see it coming. And when he does finally see it for himself, he can't even grasp it. To me, that's "You Give Love a Bad Name".

"Wanted Dead or Alive" is another song that comes out of Jon's canvas and the extremes associated with the way he saw life on the road, specifically referencing the futility of trying to keep pace with a new audience each night. It's like a gunslinger who's got someone new challenging him everyday. Richie Sambora also clearly understood the character reference and was able to put together a great cowboy look in black that captured the dark side of that heroic mythical character. A year later that image was recycled in the original Batman movie with Michael Keaton. But never was it more convincingly executed in the rock milieu than in that single iconic image of Richie, sitting on a stool, playing the intro to "Wanted, Dead or Alive."

The iconographic look of Wanted Dead or Alive

This looked like this was going to be the turning point for the band. The songs were so good (and the band so good at playing them), that the stardom we'd been chasing for three years seemed inevitable. It was just a question of producing the record and get out on the road to promote it. The label hired Bruce Fairbairn to produce the album and Bob Rock to mix it—to ensure that nothing went wrong from concept to finished product. I recall telling John it looked like he'd be adding some platinum records to the wall in his living room before too much longer.

The new album would add more platinum to Jon's living room

Jon's home office

Then came the devastating news: my dad called me in Rumson to tell me my cousin left a message for me that the DEA was rounding up the last of the Harry Feingold cocaine smuggling suspects, and that two detectives were on their way to where I worked at 240 Central Park South. It was the biggest drug bust of its time—the biggest ever on Long Island. My heart sank. I knew I had nothing to do with it, but I also knew I didn't have a convincing defense because anyone caught transporting drugs or money could claim they had no idea what they were carrying.

If anyone had been livin' on a prayer it was me. I left my first job to avoid getting killed over drugs, and my second to avoid being arrested and jailed for drugs, only to find myself in the middle of an operation so big I could get arrested, jailed or killed—without even knowing what I had done. I thought about running away—but I'd lose my percentage of the band and still have this hanging over my head. The bottom line was, it was over.

I left Rumson, picked up a bottle of Jack Daniels and headed into the office where I would wait for the cops. In a way, I was almost relieved. For the sake of my mental health, I needed the Harry Feingold nightmare—a nightmare that had been following me since I left there—to be over. I got to the office and headed upstairs with a briefcase full of video tapes of the Bon Jovi shows we'd taped under my arm. It was Saturday and even Julie wasn't in. I'd put away half the bottle by then and was about to put away the other half watching videos and lamenting every bad decision I'd ever made. But what did I do wrong? I left the limo business when I found out what was going on there. And I never would have gotten the job with Bon Jovi had I not worked at there in the first place. It was all making my head spin. But what happened next was simply beyond belief.

It was a little before 2 o'clock when there was a knock at the door. I felt the blood run right out of my face as I saw two plainclothes detectives holding their badges up to the peephole as they announced, "May we come in?" As I opened the door, they asked to see some ID and I reached back for my wallet and presented my license. After a long pause they asked me if I knew where Art Voyeisk was. Art was as straight a shooter as I had ever met. What could they want with him? I couldn't believe he could be mixed up with any of Doc's or Harry's drug businesses. They asked to look around, but even half-comatose on Jack Daniels I had the presence of mind to say, "Sorry, I just work here, can't do it," and they just turned around and left!

As it turned out, Art was the courier in Harry's million-dollar-a-week cocaine smuggling operation! Unfuckingbelievable!! I didn't even know Harry knew Art. But Art had been doing Harry's business right out of Doc's office. And since the office had been wiretapped because they were after Doc too, they had him cold.

Harry recruited Art for the job sometime after I had left Harry's limo company and while I was working for Doc. But I hadn't seen Art in months while I was on the road, and he kept his business with Harry between himself and Harry, so I had absolutely no idea what was going on. Art had been making weekly trips to Miami with cash and coming back with an average of eight pounds of cocaine each trip. In New York, if you're caught with one ounce of cocaine you can get life. But Art had been caught months earlier, made a deal, and was out on bail. Now the DEA had finished gathering everyone's testimony and was rounding everyone up for sentencing. By agreeing to testify against Feingold, Art was able to plead a lesser charge and got 2-6 years instead of 2 consecutive life sentences. So Art, the least likely guy to get involved with drugs, was sent up to do 2-6 years hard time.

But two years down the road, after the "Slippery When Wet" tour, Art would be out

NEWSDAY, SUNDAY, FEBRUARY 9, 1986

police believe that cocaine was taken — Harry decided to establish a warehouse. He talked to his oldest friend, Tommy Cahill, a New York City sanitation worker who lived with his wife and four children on Center Chicot Avenue. A deal was struck: Harry would keep his inventory in a locked attache case in a locked part of Cahill's basement, near his woodworking shop. He would also keep a triple-beam scale and a device to heat-seal bags. He would have unlimited access to the basement.

Ovetsky, known as Art flew to Miami three times a month to pick up the shipment supplied by Irving Feingold.

worked occasionally for a restaurant, traveled out of the country for special catering jobs, even won an award as "Chef of the Year" from a culinary institute. Irving, who was known as Chick, flashed money and jewelry, acquaintances said. He seemed to get a thrill from the cocaine trade. In fact, said police, he wanted to expand the business. They turned up a source who said that Irving had talked about importing more cocaine and hiding it in bags of baking flour.

Feingold kept careful books. He used a small black notebook, seized the night of his arrest, to keep track of his inventory and his profits. It shows that his profit in one 6-month period was more than half a million dollars. His last shipment arrived on March 11, 1985. He paid $33,150 for each of three kilograms, the book shows. One was sold whole for $40,000. The second was divided seven ways and sold for a total of about $50,000. The third was sold in smaller amounts — 822 grams went for $41,000, and the remaining 170 grams were seized at Cahill's house.

support his own habit. He loved the social benefits of being at the center of the cocaine subculture.

Harry and Irving Feingold had two conversational styles when they talked on the phone, according to detectives. One sounded like a father and son discussing sports and family affairs. The other had the cryptic quality of two men discussing something illegal.

"No, I'm still waiting," Irving said. "I have a very nice dinner for him."

Art took the next flight, and Irving reported to his son, "The guest has arrived."

Marc was living in the bedroom in which he had slept since he was 3. The room was papered with Playboy centerfolds, and there was a fishtank. But the most important item was a padlocked toolbox. Its contents were coveted by Marc's telephone callers — dozens on a typical night, according to detectives who were listening in.

Based on estimates by authorities who say that an average user of cocaine might buy two grams a week, Harry Feingold's cocaine eventually could have been reaching more than 3,000 people a week. That estimate, however, does not take into account that Feingold's large-scale customers were also users, and that their sales figures, unlike Feingold's, were not available to the police.

"It was the efficiency of this — to do this week in and week out," said Perini. "It ran as smooth

"I saw him all the time. I knew he was a cop," Marc said of the detective. "I didn't know he was watching me. I thought he was out socially."

And Marc had a $1,000-a-week habit. He was

On Labor Day weekend, 1982, Harry had been driving in Brightwaters when he was stopped by officers who had given him a summons two weeks earlier for driving without a license. This time, the officers found 14 pounds of marijuana and $25,000 in cash. Harry pleaded guilty to a drug charge and remained free before sentencing while his lawyers argued before an appellate court that the police had conducted an unlawful search and seizure. The case would hang over him for more than two years. But Harry Feingold made no career change.

The Harry Feingold bust was the biggest of its time—eventually implicating over 70 people

of jail. Jon and I traveled to the upstate correctional facility where Art was doing his time, and took Art to a nearby high school, where we all put on an anti-drug assembly for the kids in the school. On the strength of Jon's appearance with Art, Art was released after two years on good behavior, got on the straight and narrow, and never looked back. When Jon and I flew back to New York, Jon and I started talking about how we could both relate to what Art was telling the kids at that school. We both watched Art, standing up there in handcuffs and wearing a prison-issue uniform, tell the kids this: "When you're a teenager and you want a car or spending money, there's a temptation to get involved with drugs because you think you'll make some fast and easy money and everything will be fine. But it really won't. The truth is, most people get caught, and this is what happens."

I told Jon about how every step I took to get away from the drug business seemed to take me deeper into it. From the Columbia experience with Byrdski, to the limo experience with Harry, and now to the rock and roll business with Doc and Glen French, I had everyone in the DEA suspecting I was trafficking drugs when I never did. And just being the front man in a rock band was enough to attract the attention of law enforcement everywhere for Jon. Together, we were always targets. That's when Jon told me about when he was in high school and just got his driver's license. He needed cash and bought a pound of pot to sell. He had just driven over the Raritan Bridge between Woodbridge and Sayreville when he was pulled over by a cop for a routine traffic violation. "I had the stuff for about a half-hour, and already I was pulled over," Jon said. Luckily, he didn't have to open the trunk, and the cop never found it. But he told me every minute he was there on the side of the road seemed like an eternity. The experience of being that close to being caught just minutes after having it in his car was enough to convince Jon to never be involved with drugs again. And our experience with Art upstate forever reinforced his resistance to them.

But I'm getting ahead of myself. For almost two years leading up to the "Slippery When Wet" tour, I had been literally living on a prayer. And now, as we started the "Slippery When Wet" tour and the DEA determined that I wasn't a cocaine courier after all, I felt I had been reborn. And as I looked ahead, for the first time in quite a while, I had the optimistic feeling that the band was going to make it, and I would be with them when they did!

SLIPPERY WHEN WET

In late March 1986, the band and I moved to Vancouver for five months along with Bob Rock and Bruce Fairbairn to record the album that was eventually called "Slippery" When Wet. Recording began at Little Mountain Sound Studios in Vancouver, British Columbia, Canada, on April 6 of '86. The guys all loved Vancouver because it was far from home and full of gorgeous girls.

One month into production, we were sending back to NY rough tapes from Vancouver in order to come up with a final song selection and a name for the album, and I remember Jordan telling me that kids loved the songs and that with this album Bon Jovi would "...find a permanent place in every fan's heart." Thus it was his recommendation that the album be called Close to the Heart with a close-up visual of a fresh, bloody "Bon Jovi" tattoo cut into a busty female fan's chest. "I liked the idea because it brought real meaning to the Bon Jovi brand positioning at the precise moment in the band's history when they started turning out what would become classic hit songs," remarked Stanley. "Tattoos were just going mainstream in 1986 pop-culture,

Tico was part metronome, part machine, and all power

and I saw lots of 18+ year old girls going out to get their Bon Jovi tattoo with this new album cover—which I thought was a great way to permanently establish the band in pop culture. But it's hard to sell a concept like that over the phone, and that's what I tried to do when Doc and Jon called me from Vancouver to ask for my thoughts on the album title."

Ultimately, Jon bought the "Slippery" When Wet concept which Jordan felt was just a "one-dimensional titty joke good for a smirk in the back row of detention class, but bankrupt of any kind of enduring meaning." What's more, once the censors killed the cover, we didn't even have the "titty," just the "joke." Why was that important? "The band missed its seminal opportunity to be taken seriously, and in some ways has been paying for that decision for 20 years. Look, it's not like a different cover would have changed the music or the number of albums sold, but I still regret that I was unable to convince the guys to not go with the

"Slippery When Wet" title because this was the album that defined the Bon Jovi brand to the world. Indeed, "Slippery" had hits and plenty of them. But getting everyone to take the band seriously would be a challenge for many years to come.

At the end of July, the band had just finished a two-week tour in Canada, and we all headed back to New York for Doc and Wendy's wedding before going to Japan. This was a real high point for all of us. We had just finished what we believed to be a great hit album, and were preparing to go out on a huge tour. Even though we were opening for .38 Special, there were strong signals from the label and from the research that had been done that the band would be headlining once the album was released; the stardom of headlining was imminent.

It was one of those perfect early August days, nice and warm, but just cloudy enough to protect you from the blistering sun. Doc and Wendy's wedding reception was aboard one of the Eastern Star Cruise boats docked at Pier 61 at Chelsea Piers, NYC. Mötley was there, Bon Jovi was there and even Jon's mom and dad made it. My fiancée Patti had gotten to know Wendy very well over the past couple years. Neither of us ever recall seeing her without a smile on her face—even during those very early days when everything was rough and

Doc and Wendy's wedding boat at Chelsea Pier

nothing was certain. She was definitely one very good thing that happened to Doc, and a grounding force that may have kept him from going off the edge.

Doc and Wendy declared man and wife

The wedding ceremony and reception took place onboard the boat while we cruised the Hudson and around Manhattan. So there was plenty of time to party and catch up with everyone whom I hadn't seen for the past year or so. My best friend, Richie Fisher, had been Mötley Crüe's tour manager for almost three years and they had already been headlining for a couple years at that point, so I spent a little time talking to him about what to expect when Bon Jovi started headlining. Since Mötley was headlining, they had a bigger budget. He was able to hire an accountant, more security guards and valets so that all he had to concentrate on was taking care of the band, getting them to their venues and then to their hotel. In some ways his job was easier than mine. But I knew his band was out of control. What they do when they're awake is party. When they're too tired to party, they sleep. But Richie's concern was that at any time, instead of going to sleep, any one of them would just die or kill somebody, and there was nothing he or anyone else could do about it. So he made his job a) get the band to the gig, b) get the band to the hotel after the gig, and c) get them what they want while he was doing "a" and "b," and writing checks the next

You don't manage Mötley Crüe—you just mop up behind them

Bon Jovi played Doc and Wendy's first dance together

Heather, Jon's mom Carol and Tommy

Ally Sheedy and Dorothea at Wendy's shower…
Ally and Richie S broke up before the wedding

Tommy Lee, Dorothea, Jon and Jon's mom and dad

Richie Sambora's date Heather, Patti, Alec, Tico and Jon's dad stay close to the bar

Wendy with Jon's dad at the wedding reception

Wendy and Patti

day for anything they destroyed along the way. Richie said, "You don't manage Mötley Crüe. You just mop up behind them."

The most memorable part of the evening was that Doc kept the boat out for two hours overtime; and when we returned to the pier, our original spot had been taken by another boat. So we didn't know where we were or where our limo was. At this point it was just Doc and Wendy and me and my fiancé Patti, wandering around the desolate docks looking for our car. Suddenly, Tommy and Vince came zipping by us in our limo yelling "Fuck you!" at the tops of their lungs—they had hijacked our limo and were letting us know they knew it in their own inimitable style. We had to admit, it was fucking hilarious. We managed to cab it up to the Plaza where the four of us closed the bar and continued up in our rooms until dawn.

It was close to daybreak on the 3rd when Doc leaned over and told me I was going to be subpoenaed by the North Carolina prosecutor regarding Doc's role in smuggling 20 tons of pot into North Carolina aboard a freighter—because at that time I had been working for him setting up the Florida office. He leaned in and asked me what I was going to tell them when they deposed me, and I told him, "Whatever you want me to say." He just gave me a nod and nothing more needed to be said. I had unconditionally vowed my loyalty and would remain true to my word. And when the time came, I had forgotten virtually everything Doc ever said about pot, and everything I heard or overheard at the Florida office. From my experience setting up the Florida office and being there through the beginning, Doc and I had spent months together. I knew who called and why, and I knew some details which if disclosed may have been very incriminating to Doc, considering the charges against him. I gave them nothing more to go on than what they had gotten from their direct wiretaps. But I'm not sure what would have happened to me had there been an ounce of doubt in my voice that August night when I answered him.

When "Slippery When Wet" was released two weeks later, Bon Jovi was the opening act for .38 Special for a 3-week stint in Japan and Germany. But once the record came out it shot up the charts and we got the official go-ahead that we would be headlining. The show was all prepped and ready to go at that point because we pretty much knew it was going to happen, but everyone was waiting for the validation of record sales.

Wayne Isham made the "Slippery" videos 'iconic'

It was going to be a big change. The tour grew from 5 people to 52—with a G-1 airplane, 3 buses and 6 tractor trailer trucks. Because we were going to be headlining, the size of the stage increased dramatically—48 feet wide by 44 feet deep, with two wings each 12 feet by 32 feet, and recessed 4 feet downstage. Our first three videos were in the can, shot by Wayne Isham whose visual sensibilities were a perfect match to the songs.

We were still flying commercial planes during our first trip to Japan on the "Slippery" tour, and on one of those all-night trans-pacific trips from Tokyo to JFK on Northwest, we were all in a partying mood. The plane was at least ¾ full, with a lot of Japanese nationals aboard. And what the Japanese folks like to do on trips like this is to take a few Xanax, put

David and Jon board flight to JFK... Tico was about to shave 80 passengers

on their slippers and happi coats and just sleep right through. It can piss you off because you can't even get comfortable, and meanwhile, they can't wake up.

While Jon and Richie had all the attention of the entirely female crew, Tico, having problems getting a drink from the preoccupied crew, decided to have a little fun of his own with a full can of shaving cream and razor. While they were asleep, Tico went from one passenger to another—every one he could reach from the aisle that was sound asleep—shaving off their eyebrows. By the time he ran out of shaving cream, Tico had shaved the eyebrows off some 80 people on the plane who were too knocked out to know what was going on. Richie, Jon and I became aware of what was going on when we looked at Richie Sambora's face as he walked back from the lavatory at the front of the plane and saw all these bald faces and eyebrows looking back at him on the way back to his seat—more than 80 people with little streaks of shaving cream where their eyebrows used to be. But the best part was when they all woke up and began looking at each other and then at our group, looking for the culprit. By that time Tico was sound asleep, and had completely averted suspicion as having been the perpetrator.

We were back in New York on September 2, and all Jon talked about was getting out and driving the Ferrari he bought at the end of the first tour. It was a Ferrari alright, but it constantly broke down and was virtually undriveable. But Jon had had it repaired while we were away and he was really looking forward to driving it. Jon told me when he got home he would swing by and pick me up. No sooner had he picked me up and we headed out, than the car farted, burped and died right there. We just took the plates off and took a cab back to my house where we grabbed my car and proceeded to drive to the city, and Jon bought a brand new red Ferrari with tan interior right on the spot. I never saw the old one again.

Before we set out on the "Slippery" headlining tour, the band, Doc and I made a trip to Memphis to visit Graceland. Presley, his parents Gladys and Vernon Presley, and his grandmother, are buried there in what is called the "Meditation Gardens." For me it was a particularly moving experience, because Jon always wanted to be Elvis and felt a deep connection to him that was intensified as he was about to embark on the "Slippery" tour. As I led everyone through the gardens, the same place where Elvis himself would often go to reflect on important matters that he was about to face in his life, Jon stopped, paused, and in complete silence stared down to where Elvis was buried as if to channel him while contemplating the months ahead. Seeing that and being there for that was one of the most spiritual experiences of my life.

A pilgrimage to Graceland before heading off to our first headlining tour—"Slippery" When Wet

As we went on the road to promote "Slippery" in Australia and the States, it was hard not to get swept up in the euphoria of headlining and the anticipation of success. By this time, we had traded our bus for a G-1 jet and our crew had grown from just a handful of people to 52. And instead of pulling the show behind us in a Ryder trailer, the show traveled in six full-sized tractor-trailer trucks. The show was a huge investment and was 100% world class.

On a headlining tour, everything changes because it's your tour. So you have to see to every detail. For example, there are dozens of venue specifications:

L. No discrimination for reason of race, religion, age, sex, or country of national origin shall be permitted or authorized by Purchaser in connection with the sale of tickets or admission to or seating accommodations at the engagement.

X. GROUND TRANSPORTATION

A. Purchaser will be contacted by Richard Bozzett with ground transportation requirements.

XI. MINIMUM MAN POWER REQUIREMENTS

A. Union/non - union requirements

1. Calls
   a. Rigging call 08:00

      3 riggers
      1 ground man
      4 loaders
      1 electric
      6 stage hands
      1 forklift with operator

   b. Stage call 09:00

      add twelve (12) stagehands for a total of eighteen (18)
      add one (1) forklift with operator for a total of two (2).

   c. Show call: time TBA

      8 hands on deck
      1 electrician
      1 house lights man
      1 forklift with operator
      12 spotlight operators (8 in house; 4 on truss, climbing required)

   d. Out call: time TBA

      22 stage hands
      3 riggers
      1 ground man
      8 loaders (where possible, to do more than one truck at a time otherwise, 4
      2 forklifts with operators

B. Stage Size: 48 feet wide X 44 feet deep. Stage must be five or six feet height.

C. Sound Wings:
   1. stage right: 12 feet wide X 32 feet deep at same height as stage but recessed 4 feet from downstage.
   2. stage left: 12 feet wide X 32 feet deep at same height as stage but recessed 4 feet from downstage.

It may be just "rock 'n roll," but it's not for people who are uncomfortable with the "details":

D. Barricade: BON JOVI carries and will supply their own barricade. It is approximately 70 feet wide, 4 feet high, flush on the downstage edge of thrust and is freestanding and self supporting.

E. Thrust: BON JOVI carries a portable aluminum grating thrust that is attached the downstage edge of the promoter provided stage. It is 14 feet wide, and to 14 feet at the apex.

F. Chair Placement: Subsequent to section B and C, the first 50 feet of arena floor, plus a lane 20 feet wide to the mix position must be kept clear of chairs and other obstructions until cleared by production manager.

G. House Mixing Risers: Riser dimensions shall be 16 feet wide X 24 feet deep X 2 feet high for halls with reserved seating, or X 1 feet high if general admission. Exact placement shall be center of house, 100 feet from stage. A free standing barricade completely surrounding riser is also required because of artist's performance at the riser halfway through the show.

H. Spotlights:

  1. one of the following

    a. 8 super troopers
    b. 8 xenon super troopers
    c. 8 gladiators

  A combination of the above is acceptable upon approval by production manager. All spotlights must be in perfect working order. Positioning of spotlights shall be determined on day of show.

I. Stage Lights: to be supplied by artist

J. Sound: to be supplied by artist

K. Minimum Power Requirements

  1. Lights

    a. 1 X 800 AMP ,3 phase, 4 wire (or a combination of the equivalent i.e. 600 X 2 etc.)

  2. Sound

    a. 1 X 400 AMP, 3 phase, 4 wire service

  3. Rigging, Fog Machine, and Hydraulics, 200 AMP 3 phase

  4. Crew Buses

    a. 3 X 50 AMP shore power services if possible

If power is located more than 75 feet from upstage right, Purchaser will supply necessary cable and proper lugs.

Here, for example is the light rigging plot along with the specifications for lights, sound, special effects—even a spec for what drinks are needed on stage:

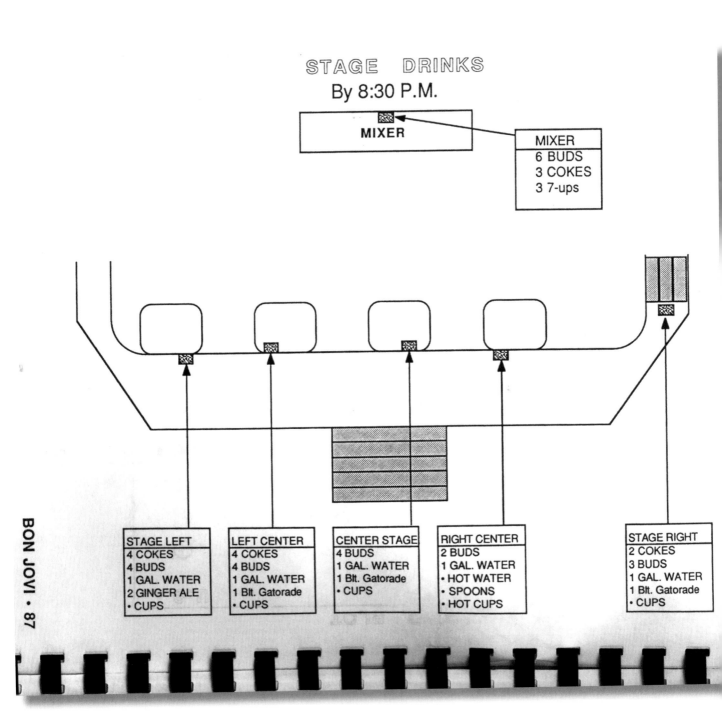

Hell , there's even a specification for the band's snacks before the show:

BAND CATERING
Placed in Band's Room

By 4:30 P.M.

FOOD:

- ❑ One small veggy tray with dip.
- ❑ Hot soup creamy or broth style.
- ❑ Local favorite (meat or fish).
- ❑ Salad (no cucumbers) • Thousand Island, Itailian, & Ranch.
- ❑ Fruit bowl plus 3 lemons and 3 limes • (knife).
- ❑ 1 $\frac{1}{2}$ cups of fresh squeezed lemon juice.
- ❑ Salt and pepper.

Serves **10**

By 3:00 P.M.

DRINKS:

- ❑ 10 bottles Evian Water.
- ❑ 3 bottles Lemonade Gatorade.
- ❑ 3 bottles Lime Gatorade.
- ❑ 18 cans Country Time Lemonade.
- ❑ 6 cans Diet Coke.
- ❑ 6 cans Lipton Ice Tea with Lemon.
- ❑ 6 cans Jolt.
- ❑ 6 cans Canada Dry Gingerale.
- ❑ 6 cans Canada Dry Wild Cherry.
- ❑ 1/2 gallon natural orange juice.
- ❑ 1 case Budweiser.
- ❑ 1 quart cranberry juice.
- ❑ 1 gallon whole milk.
- ❑ 2 quarts chocolate milk.
- ❑ Hot tea service • (Lipton Decaf Tea Bags).
- ❑ Coffee service • (sugar & honey).

BON JOVI • 87

With "Slippery" When Wet, we said goodbye to the old the old flash pots, and brought in real pyro, and you obviously need to carry licenses for that.

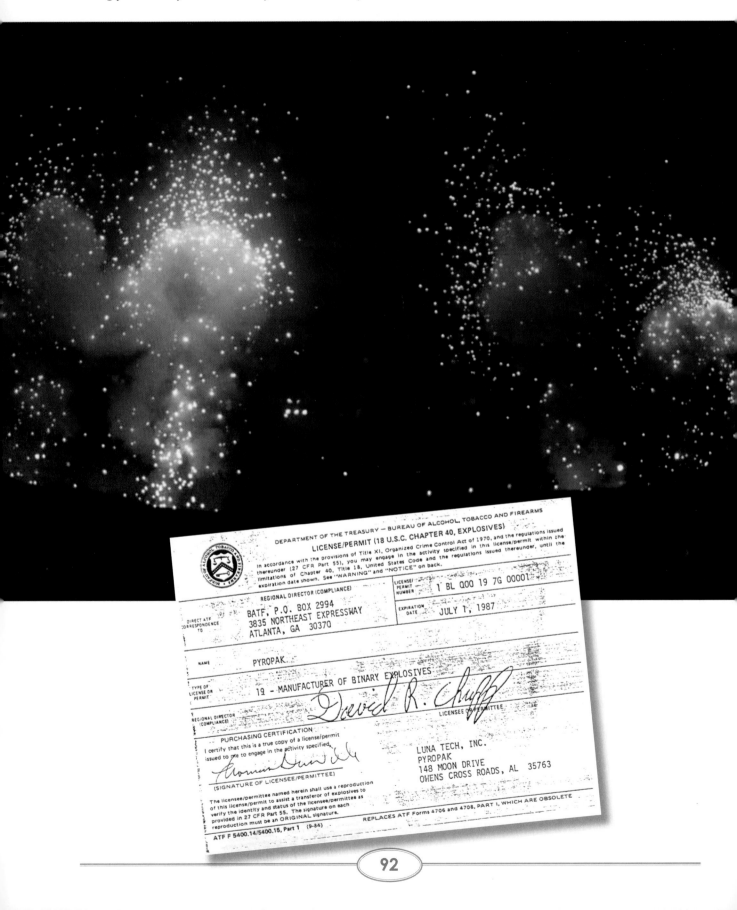

When you're on the road you have to stop by the local radio stations that are promoting the show and playing your records to do interviews. On the way out, they typically ask you to cut a few promos. You have to write the spots on the fly and get back to the hotel or the venue as soon as possible. Jon always cut his spots to time the first time. Here are a few of the hand-written notes we would write in the car, on the way to the stations or right on the spot:

HEY - THIS IS BON JOVI & YOU'RE LISTENIN' TO KANSAS CITY'S ORIGINAL ROCK N ROLL STATION - KY 102

HI - THIS BON JOVI & YOU'RE LISTENIN' TO PENN-SYLVANIA'S CAPITAL OF ROCK N ROLL - WHTF

HI - THIS IS BON JOVI - I'M IN TOWN - I'll KNOW WHEN I GET...

THIS IS BON JOVI & YOU'RE CRUISIN WITH SPRINGFIELD'S FINE TUNED ROCK N ROLL MACHINE - WYMG

LA AINT GOT NUTHIN ON SANTA BARBARA - THIS IS HEAVEN ON EARTH - BON JOVI HERE ON K-TIDE - KTYD

TOM CALE - ARE YOU AWAKE YET ?! ..... WAKE UP - THIS IS BON JOVI ON SACRAMENTO'S KZAP !

KRDJ - FRESNO'S ROCK N ROLL IS SLIPPERY WHEN WET WITH BON JOVI !

Hi THIS IS BON JOMBO & I LIKE TO RIDE FAT WOMEN WITH MR. BILL IN ATLANTA & CRANK UP 96 ROCK

Hi THIS IS Phil in The Bronx AND YOUR LISTENIN TO 96 Rock ATLANTA'S PURE Rock & Roll

HI, THIS IS BON JOVI - YOU'RE ROCKIN WITH LANSING'S LAZER 92 - WLNZ !

Hi this is Jon Bon Jovi and your listening to New England's' 10 hits in-a-row radio station, 92. ~~PRO~~ PRO-7-M

Hi this is JB and stay tuned to 92 for details on how to win ~~backstage~~ backstage passes to the hottest show on earth only on 92 PRO-7M

Four Seasons Hotels

Within weeks of its release, the album was number 1. Only 12 months ago, it was a challenge to get a radio station to interview us, but suddenly we had the entire media world descending upon us. We were about to embark on the ride of a lifetime and we knew it.

Bon Jovi was not just a hit band; it was everywhere you looked. In one fell swoop, it had transcended pop culture. Shows sold out within hours of being announced. Between family, friends and celebrities, the after-show guest list was as high as 500. When you're suddenly opening in 20,000 seat venues, the influx of cash is staggering and immediately life-changing. A sold out headliner tour supporting a #1 album can generate a half million dollars a night in ticket revenue and merchandise for the band alone.

During the Runaway tour, each member of the band was earning $250 per week. From the beginning of the 7800 tour until the time the "Slippery" tour got underway, each member of the band was earning $750 per week. Suddenly the band was making money, and Jon, Doc and Polygram in particular were making ridiculous sums of money.

The band came off salary and started earning a percentage of retail record sales. Richie and Tico got 1%, and David and Alec got .5%. Doc got 20%, the accountants got 10%, and the rest went to Jon. If you didn't already know that Jon believed he alone was Bon Jovi and that the rest of the band members were simply hired musicians, the percentages outlined above ratify the point. If you go by the numbers, Jon was 50 times more important than Richie or Tico, and 100 times more important than David and Alec. There is no other way to interpret them.

(1)

BON JOVI PRODUCTIONS
c/o McGhee Entertainment, Inc.
240 Central Park South
Suite 2C
New York, New York 10019

As of September 26, 1986

(1)

Mr. Alec John Such
1046 Truxton Drive
Perth Amboy, New Jers

Dear Alec:

When signed by yo
all services rendered by
with the recording of
musical group professio
"Album") for PolyGram
musician or otherwise in
recordings embodying tl
(iii) the exclusive use b
whatsoever including, w
any or all formats (witl
media, motion pictures
and (iv) all services re
connection with the pro

1.   (a)   In full
or otherwise in connecti
will pay to you:

(i)   Ir
hereby acknowledged), v
States of the Album, a
price (the "basic royalty

(ii)   T
and other sales of the A
payable by PRI to us for
territory in respect of t
Agreement").

(iii)   A
calculated, and paid in t
sales, retail list price,
determined, calculated (

(iv)   Ir
reflects that royalties .
statement is accompan

BON JOVI PRODUCTIONS
c/o McGhee Entertainment, Inc.
240 Central Park South
Suite 2C
New York, New York 10019

As of September 26, 1986

Mr. David Rashbaum
103 Thomas Place
Edison, New Jersey 08837

Dear David:

When signed by you and us, the following shall constitute our agreement with respect to (i)
all services rendered by you at any time as a musician, composer or otherwise in connection
with the recording of the master recordings (the "Masters") embodied on the album by the
musical group professionall   and entitled "Slippery When Wet" (the
"Album") for PolyGram Rec   by you at any time as a
musician or otherwise in cor   udiovisual
recordings embodying the p
(iii) the exclusive use by u
whatsoever including, with
any or all formats (with o
media, motion pictures anc
and (iv) all services rend
connection with the promo

1.   (a)   In full c
or otherwise in connectio
will pay to you:

(i)   Ir
hereby acknowledged), v
States of the Album, a
price (the "basic royalty

(ii)
and other sales of the ,
payable by PRI to us f
territory in respect o
Agreement").

(iii)
calculated, and paid
sales, retail list pr
determined, calculat

(iv
reflects that royalt
statement is acco

BON JOVI PRODUCTIONS
c/o McGhee Entertainment, Inc.
240 Central Park South
Suite 2C
New York, New York 10019

As of September 26, 1986

(1)

Mr. Richie Sambora
128 Harriet Street
Woodbridge, New Jersey 07095

Dear Richie:

When signed by you and us, the
all services rendered by you at any
with the recording of the master
musical group professionally knowi
"Album") for PolyGram Records, Inc
musician or otherwise in connection
recordings embodying the performa
(iii) the exclusive use by us of you
whatsoever including, without limit
any or all formats (with or without
media, motion pictures and any othe
and (iv) all services rendered by y
connection with the promotional tou

1.   (a)   In full consideratio
or otherwise in connection with the ,
will pay to you:

(i)   In addition tc
hereby acknowledged), with respect
States of the Album, a royalty of or
royalty rate").

(ii)   The royalty p
and other sales of the Album shall be
payable by PRI to us for net sales o
territory in respect of the Album is
Agreement").

(iii)   All royalties
calculated, and paid in the same ma
sales, retail list price, reserves,
determined, calculated and paid purs

(iv)   If any semi-
reflects that royalties are due to t
statement is accompanied by a pc

BON JOVI PRODUCTIONS
c/o McGhee Entertainment, Inc.
240 Central Park South
Suite 2C
New York, New York 10019

As of September 26, 1986

Mr. Tico Torres
426 Stanley Place
Rahway, New Jersey 07065

Dear Tico:

When signed by you and us, the following shall constitute our agreement with respect to (i)
all services rendered by you at any time as a musician, composer or otherwise in connection
with the recording of the master recordings (the "Masters") embodied on the album by the
musical group professionally known as "Bon Jovi" and entitled "Slippery When Wet" (the
"Album") for PolyGram Records, Inc. ("PRI"); (ii) all services rendered by you at any time as a
musician or otherwise in connection with the creation and production of any and all audiovisual
recordings embodying the performances of any musical compositions contained on the Album;
(iii) the exclusive use by us of your name, image, likeness and performances in any manner
whatsoever including, without limitation, use on or in connection with phonograph records in
any or all formats (with or without visual images), broadcasts or other transmissions in any
media, motion pictures and any other method, means or media now known or hereafter derived;
and (iv) all services rendered by you as a performer, musician and member of Bon Jovi in
connection with the promotional tour (the "Tour") in support of the Album.

1.   (a)   In full consideration of all services rendered by you at any time as a musician
or otherwise in connection with the Album, the Tour and of all rights granted by you herein, we
will pay to you:

(i)   In addition to your union scale payments (receipt of which payments is
hereby acknowledged), with respect to net sales through normal retail channels in the United
States of the Album, a royalty of one (1%) percent of the suggested retail list price (the "basic
royalty rate").

(ii)   The royalty payable to you for foreign sales, budget records, club sales
and other sales of the Album shall be reduced in the same proportion that the basic royalty rate
payable by PRI to us for net sales of the Album through normal retail channels in the particular
territory in respect of the Album is reduced pursuant to our agreement with PRI (the "Artist
Agreement").

(iii)   All royalties payable to you hereunder shall be computed, determined,
calculated, and paid in the same manner (e.g., container charges, free goods, definition of net
sales, retail list price, reserves, etc.) as royalties payable to us by PRI are computed,
determined, calculated and paid pursuant to the Artist Agreement.

(iv)   If any semi-annual accounting statement received by us from PRI
reflects that royalties are due to us with respect to net sales of the Album, and such PRI
statement is accompanied by a payment in said amount, we shall within thirty (30) days

Alec's theatrical energy and soulfulness have been conspicuously absent since he left

An infallible beat, raw power and superhuman endurance are the Tico trademarks

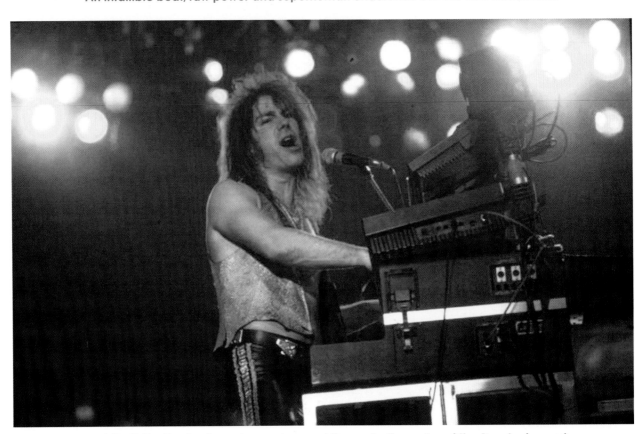

David's distinctive keyboards are always at the melodic center of the Bon Jovi sound

It was all good for now, but when each of the band members walked out and went his own way at the end of the New Jersey tour two years later (bringing about the unofficial end of the band), it would be the stark reality of this math that was at the center of everyone's dissent. Plus, by that point, everyone was just plain exhausted from touring.

Though my primary allegiance was to Jon and Doc who were paying me, I was close to everyone in the band. And it bothered me that the individual band member's contributions to the success of the band were not being taken into consideration in any way close to being "fair." This was a band driven by live performance and each one was holding up his end. Yet they were still being paid like they were just recruited for "Jon's band." When I was given the proposed agreements in August, I questioned the thinking behind them and refused to present them to the band. Taking nothing away from Jon's role in starting the band and driving the performance, it seemed to me the proposed agreements barely recognized the importance of the live show and touring. When I brought the issue up to Doc, he was quick to point out this was not his call and certainly not mine. I conceded that point, but I told Doc I believed this could lead to an eventual meltdown of the band, and that I wanted my percentage to be worth something.

If this was all Jon's idea, I didn't think it was based on greed, rather on the antiquated notion that he put the band together and everyone else was "for hire." But I told Doc that it was our job to get Jon reoriented to the reality of that moment—that this was a band driven by live performance and touring, and everyone was pulling his end. My point of view was that Jon needed people like us to tell him the truth because the bigger the star, the bigger the bullshit around him, and that Jon would appreciate that. But Doc was adamant about what he perceived to be the practical aspects of a situation. If this was the way Jonny wanted it, why argue? What's the percentage in arguing the point and quite possibly appearing "subversive"? You end up looking like an outsider and you get cut off. But I was the one who saw how everybody worked to make the live show what it was, and I was concerned that Jon would see the error in his math too late, and that the guys would end up so pissed off that they might leave and never come back.

In retrospect it may have been a bad idea for me to push the issue because it probably did make me look "subversive" to Doc instead of "supportive" of him. And who knows how he would spin it to make me look like the asshole if I pushed the idea. In any business it's easy to find an asshole who's willing to veto common sense in favor of puckering up to kiss the boss' ass. Maybe I would have done the same if I were the one earning 20% on everything. Who knows?

The most mind-boggling experience was coming home and playing NY and Jersey. Home town shows were simply a mad house of media and business buzz and fan hysteria. The backstage guest list started looking like a who's who of celebs and other high profile people who wanted to be part of what was happening. When we came back to play the Meadowlands at home, we'd sell out 4 or 5 days in a row and there would be pandemonium managing back stage passes. Just family alone would require hundreds of backstage passes. Add to that friends and promoters, radio and celebs and we would have literally thousands and thousands of requests for backstage passes and the capacity to handle only about 5% of that. You have to tell a lot of people "no," and you just hate to.

After one of our home town shows at the Nassau Coliseum in April, I saw Howard Stern in the backstage area with one of his three daughters. This was years before he made a movie, did any pay-per-view or wrote any books, and was not yet the "King of all Media." However, at the time Howard was the coolest and most popular morning drive personality here in New York, and had been one of the earliest supporters of the band. Everyone in

the crew and most everyone in the band loved listening to him whenever we were in town or in a city like Philadelphia where his syndicated program ran. Even then, Howard had sufficient celebrity status to get himself into any band's hospitality area—the backstage area for radio contest winners, friends and family—but it was wall-to-wall and I knew that the band wouldn't be coming out to Hospitality that night. I'm not sure he recognized me even though we had met several times when I took Jon to interviews with him at WNBC in 1984 and WXRK in 1985, but he spotted my badge and asked me if I could get his daughter back to the dressing room. This was Howard, one of the band's heroes, so I dropped everything and took both of them back for a photo-op with Jon and the band. I was struck by the fact that outside the radio station he just seemed like a regular guy trying to do something special for his daughter. He was just as professional and gracious as anyone could be, and his daughter was just ecstatic about having met Jon.

Afterwards, I escorted them back to Hospitality and was quickly overwhelmed by a backlog of other guest matters. I knew Howard well-enough to know that once he had met

Jon feeds off the adulation of the crowd and gives always gives 110% back

with the band he just wanted to get out of there. But Howard made a point of making his way all the way back to me through wall-to-wall people just to say "thanks" before he took off. I told him, "Anything for you, Howard," and said good night.

There's an incredible dynamic built into doing live shows—when you give everything you've got to an audience, and they know it and they give you even more energy back. You take that energy and give them more, and they take it and give you still more back. And that's the way the whole night goes—with the band trying to one-up the audience, and a

Richie played and performed with the same love and respect for the audience

grateful audience trying to tell you how much they love and appreciate it. It's a similar dynamic to drugs—a quest to keep going higher, and the band pushing themselves to keep giving to the audience beyond their capacity to give.

As a tour manager, there was nothing like being in the middle of it. During "Slippery", Doc came out to the shows more often, and I remember him doing the same thing I did—any chance we could, we would just go out into the crowd and watch everybody dig our band.

In the early days of "Slippery," I had to be back in time for Jon's wardrobe changes. We'd have approximately 45 seconds to change while he was holding a microphone. So there I was, the big tour manager with one foot against a folding chair trying to literally peel his skin tight pants off and get him into different pants and an American flag. I remember telling Jon that as soon as we had money we were going to hire a wardrobe girl because I wasn't getting paid to go eye to eye with his

love-muscle every night. But from our very first gig, through the New Jersey tour seven years later, I never missed cue and we never missed a single show, but we came close.

During the "Slippery When Wet" tour, Marlo Thomas asked us to perform the acoustic versions of "Living on a Prayer," "You give Love a Bad Name" and "Wanted: Dead or Alive" on a live satellite feed from the Hard Rock Café in NYC in support of the St Jude's

Children's Hospital opening in the Soviet Union. The show was scheduled for 7 AM the day after we'd playing Pittsburgh Pa., until after midnight.

Jon, Richie and I headed for our plane to go to NY right after the show. We took off around 1 AM and arrived in NY around 3 AM. We had a car waiting that got us to the Park Lane Hotel in midtown Manhattan around 4 AM. Jon and Richie slept for about an hour, but I was too worried about missing the show to fall asleep. At 5:30 AM I woke the guys who were still exhausted from the previous night's show. But neither of them was complaining because the cause was the only thing on their minds. We walked around the corner to the Hard Rock ready to go on at 7AM.

It was the second time they'd performed the acoustic versions of those songs, and the show went off without a hitch, laying the groundwork for Russia a year later. Then we had to fly out to Cleveland to do the 3rd show in 24 hours. But the weather took a turn for the worst, and instead of getting out of NYC by noon, we're still sitting on the tarmac at 3:30 PM.

The tower, aware of our plight, gave us the go-ahead to take off a little after 4 PM, but we encountered further weather-related delays trying to land in Cleveland. By the time we touched down in Cleveland, the opening act had already gone 20 minutes overtime and had wrapped. And the audience, sensing something was up, was growing impatient. As we pulled up to the backstage gates and the doors opened, everyone was waiting for us. An ecstatic production manager Paul Korzelius breathed a sigh of relief as he rushed Jon and Richie off to the dressing room. I headed off to the production room to advance that night's hotel and travel arrangements because we were leaving for Chicago right after the show. The show started virtually on-time, but Jon treated the audience to extra encores just on principle. I got on the phone with FBO to re-file our flight plan out!

As busy as Marlo Thomas was and is, she found the time to send the band a very thoughtful "thank you" note. To me it was something very special because I grew up in love with her from seeing her on TV on "That Girl." And here she was today, doing this fabulous work. It reminded me of all the real "good" in the world and thoroughly warmed my heart.

After the show, the guys headed right to the plane and passed out, before doing it all over again in Chicago the next day. But as the popularity of the band continued to grow, it became harder and harder to get out of the venues and back to our hotels. We had to use aliases at our hotels and create disguises to move out of the venues and go out after the shows. Paul Stanley had once confided that that was the best thing about Kiss. That they didn't have to put on disguises to blend in with the fans, they would simply take off their makeup and become one of them. But we had to put on costumes to blend with the crowd.

Jon had an awesome disguise that made him look like the son of some techno-geek and Groucho Marx. On no less than 30 occasions that I know of, Jon would walk right out the front door with people leaving the concert just to listen to what they were saying about him. And they didn't have a clue who he was. You could be nose to nose with him and you'd never know it.

Jon in disguise—he could walk right out the front door undetected

Richie and Tico resemble a gay dance team as they make their way out of the hotel after a show

Richie and Tico were equally convincing in their disguises as well. Everybody liked to go out into the crowd to hear what people were saying about the show. Then we'd go out after and hit a few clubs or bars if we didn't have to travel until the next day.

One night after ending up back in a bar at a Holiday Inn, I left Tico talking to some other guy as they were closing the place. Anyway, Tico came casually walking out of the bar while I was standing at the front desk arranging wake up calls for the next day, with blood just pouring down the side of his face. I said, "Tico, what the fuck happened?" He acted surprised, unfazed.

I rushed him to the hospital where they pulled out huge chunks of glass and tried to stitch him up because the blood was everywhere. Tico said, "Richie, I don't want anybody to know," and I said, "How the hell are you going to keep it a secret? Your damn head is split open like a melon and you've got stitches on one side of your head all the way from the front to the back." What happened was that he either broke a bottle over his own head to make a point or he had the other guy do it to show how tough he was. You'd have to ask Tico.

Anyway, for the next two weeks he was parting his hair on the other side and combing it over the stitches, until some 10 days later right before a show, he came up to me and told me that his head really hurt. I went back to the bathroom at the venue we were playing and took a look at the stitches only to see a thick piece of glass shaped like an arrowhead sticking out from beneath the stitches. Evidently, a piece that was deeply embedded was being rejected and was protruding from his head and busting open stitches. Well, I had the name of a doctor in every city we played and I made a call to get one down there right away because we were supposed to do a show in an hour and Tico was dying from the pain.

The doctor arrived and we went back to the bathroom to do an emergency operation to remove the glass. I can't stand the sight of blood and I was playing the role of nurse holding open the wound, with blood flying all over the place, trying to keep the blood clear. The doctor kept trying to grab the chunk of glass, but it was like part of his head by then and it wouldn't come out. Finally after digging and digging, the doctor proceeded to remove a piece of glass roughly a square inch the shape of a triangle and as thick as the bottom of a coke bottle from Tico's head!

When we came out of the bathroom, everyone in the band was waiting outside asking what happened. I said, "I'll let Tico tell you that story, but we have to be on stage in 10 minutes."

I never asked Tico what happened. The tour manager just does what has to be done.

On August 22, 1987, almost two years to the day after playing Castle Donington for the first time and eating a pound of mud, dirt, rocks and piss in plastic bottles, we came back to Donington, this time to headline. This was a huge monkey we had to get off our back, and we blew the audience away. There's nothing like the adulation of 100,000 screaming fans. Especially after taking so much shit from them just two years before.

Tico did a comb-over for two weeks to cover up his stitches

This was the performance to purge all demons, and it did. During Bon Jovi's set, Dee Snider, Bruce Dickinson and Paul Stanley joined the band to perform "We're an American Band" to a thunderous ovation.

After a show at the LA Forum, we were done with the U.S. tour and off to Doc's house in Newport Beach before heading off to Japan again. It was about a 45 minute drive from one place to the other, so everyone headed off on their own with whoever was around. I offered to take Vince Neil's and Nicki Sixx's girlfriends in my limo. These guys always had the most drop-dead gorgeous ones, and I had room for them because Jon had left for Doc's right from the stage in another car because there were too many guests. We were headed south on the 405 toward Newport Beach when the most drop-dead gorgeous one of all of them asks me to stop the car because she has to pee. We pulled over and I opened the door, but she asked me to come with her because the shoulder grade fell off sharply. I was holding her hands as she was peeing saying to myself I really do like this tour manager's job. We partied all the way to Doc's house, and didn't stop until dawn.

Before I knew it we were off for a short stint in Japan for what would be our 2nd trip there in 13 months on the "Slippery" Tour—and then off to Australia. Our first stop was Tokyo, where we were scheduled for five shows at the Budokhan. I had heard that Michael Jackson was in town to do three shows of his own and was staying at the Hotel Century Hyatt where we were staying. So I reached out to his manager to see if we could get together for a few drinks and photo-op.

The band and I with Michael Jackson and his longtime manager, Frank Dileo

We were all planning to hang out for awhile, but Michael showed up with Bubbles, the chimpanzee he adopted in the early 80's. This was around the time that people began referring to Michael as "Wacko Jacko," because he would do these bizarre inexplicable things that would leave you scratching your head wondering what the fuck he was up to. Well Michael had brought Bubbles along on his world tour and after we took a couple pictures together, he asked me if I wanted to have him come up to our hotel room. I said "sure" and got the band together in my room, and about 20 minutes later Bubbles showed up banging on the door with Michael!

When I opened the door, Bubbles came charging in, leaping from one piece of furniture to the next, as if he was shot up with espresso and Red Bull—going wild and knocking shit over—and the whole time, the son of a bitch had his hand down in his diaper playing with himself like it was his job. Finally, he just stopped running around and jacked off on Bon Jovi security guard Danny Francis' cowboy boots. And when he started picking up the jism and throwing it around, we all ran for cover. If it was anyone else's monkey, Danny would have reached over and wrung it out like a damp towel and killed it right on the spot, but he just stood motionless staring the piss-pot down as Michael stood there laughing the whole time.

The next day, there was a story floating around the hotel about how Bon Jovi "trashed their hotel room" and I remember thinking: there's no way this chimp is trashing Michael's room everyday. He must do something to him to keep him calm... Then it occurred to me.

Jon, like Michael, relied on medications to help him sleep while on tour

How do you calm down a chimp that just wants to jack-off?

The whole world was under the impression that Jackson was trying to recapture his childhood by taking Bubbles everywhere he went. But somehow I got the impression that Bubbles provided some other kind of entertainment for Michael!

Doc came out to visit us in Japan. Mötley Crüe, once the stars of McGhee Entertainment, were now taking a backseat in the press to Bon Jovi. And each member of Mötley was becoming increasingly difficult to manage. Back home, Tommy and Nikki locked all the doors of their limo as their driver got out of the car to open their door at their hotel. They drove off around the parking lot with the driver chasing them, eventually crashing into the hotel gate. That, as it turned out, was to be the mild stuff.

A week later, Nikki shot up too much heroin and overdosed in his Parker Meridian hotel room after a Mötley concert in New York.

A few days later, before a Crüe concert in Rochester, New York, Vince slammed a jar of Gulden's Dijon mustard against the backstage wall when he saw there was no French's mustard for the sandwich he was making. The smash severed tendons, nerves and an artery, almost cutting a finger off his right hand. The show was cancelled and he was airlifted to the Hand Center in Baltimore, where he had to undergo an eight-hour operation the next day.

Two days later, Steve Tyler and Joe Perry left a note on the windshield of the Crüe's tour plane, telling them that they were crashing

Doc's patience with Mötley was coming to an end

and burning and needed help. Back then, you had to be way fucked up for Aerosmith to tell you that you need help.

A week after that Nikki missed a flight for a concert because he was out of his mind on cocaine. This was followed by a band meeting at which time they confronted Nikki about his drug use. It appeared that Doc was going to need even more time with Mötley, just to keep them from killing themselves or each other. I remember Doc refusing to allow the band to begin a tour of Europe, feeling fairly certain that some of them would come back in bodybags.

This was a big change for me and everyone at McGhee—only months earlier, when I would show up at the main office at 240 Central Park South, Doc's partner, Doug Thaler would say, "Hey, Richie, where you been?" And after I told him I was on the road with Bon Jovi, he would sarcastically reply, "Bon who vi? They don't make the money around here; Mötley makes the money." I put up with that shit for a long time. But now that they were hot, Doug played it like he was with Bon Jovi all along, when in truth, during the early days, Doc and I were the only ones who believed in them.

I think it may have been a little hard for Mötley to accept Bon Jovi's success. Don't let the party image fool you. These guys were tough competitors, and after years of being cast as big brother rock and roll legends to Jon, they suddenly found themselves in the shadow of their "little brother's" success, and it may have felt to them like their time had passed. Anyway, that's what drugs can make you think. They would bounce back in '89, with the release of their Dr. Feelgood album. But for now, the bigger issue was that Doc was going to have to spend even more time with Mötley than ever before, and that meant I would have to work harder than ever to make sure Doc's absence on the Bon Jovi side wasn't conspicuous.

Between 1986 and 1987, "Slippery When Wet" produced an unprecedented string of hit singles, including three Top 10 Billboard Hot 100 hits, two of which ("You Give Love A Bad Name" and "Livin' On A Prayer") reached #1, making Bon Jovi the first hard rock band to ever have two consecutive #1 Billboard Hot 100 chart hits. "Slippery" When Wet also was the first hard rock album to spawn three Billboard Hot 100 Top 10 hits. The album also had impressive staying power, with 38 weeks inside the Billboard 200 Top 5, including 8 weeks at #1.

Our promoters in Japan were exceptional at their work—and wonderful folks to be with

What makes the difference between a great band and an iconic band? The local promoters and radio stations. These are the guys that make a band, and we did right by each and every one of them. These are the people that talk it up when you're coming to town. These are the guys who put together the contests and play the records. For some reason or another, these people really believed in us and hitched their wagon to our star. And no matter how busy or how tired we were coming into a new town on tour, we made ourselves available to get together with these people as if they were family—not just to do appearances and interviews, but to really get together and have fun. We would put together softball, pool and bowling parties—whatever suited the local people. Who went? Everybody. No special attendance requirements or constraints.

For example, when we went to Japan for the third time, we pulled together all the troops—the local radio station people, the promoter and employees, the band and crew. We're talking 40 or more people. And we all went bowling for the night. I think part of it was these people were with us from the beginning—and there is no substitute for people who believe in you before you get there.

Tico and Jon discuss their curveballs as Richie looks on

Based on the power of songs and the chance to pay off Polygram, the tour was stretched out to the edges of human endurance—an unprecedented 18 months. Yes, we actually went out on the road for a year and a half to support that album. As a result, the album had impressive staying power, with 38 weeks inside the Billboard 200 Top 5, including 8 weeks at #1. It was the best-selling album of 1987 in the United States, and eventually reached Diamond certification by the RIAA selling 28 million copies, making it the 48th best-selling album in the United States. The album peaked at number one on the U.S. Billboard 200, becoming Bon Jovi's first number-one album in United States. Over two years after its release, "Slippery When Wet" was certified twelve times platinum by the Recording Industry Association of America. In the UK, it peaked at #6, spent a total of 107 weeks inside the Top 75, 23 of them on the Top 20. It became Bon Jovi's biggest-selling studio album in the UK, achieving over 1 million copies sold, receiving a 3x Platinum certification by the BPI. The album also achieved diamond status in Canada and six times platinum status in Australia. I don't think the "Slippery When Wet" tour will ever be matched by any band or artist again. It was just one of those times when everybody knew what was expected of them and performed at a level a notch above their capabilities. It was perfectly played, perfectly staged, perfectly played out—everything done professionally, the right way—the output of many incredibly talented and dedicated people.

Dorothea, Jon, Stacy, Richie, Doc and Wendy hiking down to the water in Hawaii

We finished the tour in Japan in mid-October and then headed off to Hawaii for a few shows and a 2-week Hawaiian vacation. Jon surprised me with a new BMW as a "thank you" for my work on the tour. It was especially gratifying because he had just taken a huge hit days before. On "Black Monday," October 19, 1987, the day stock markets around the world crashed, shedding a huge value in a very short time. But I was waiting for the big payday I had earned from Doc, who had promised me 5 percentage points of his end in exchange for me managing the band on the road. And his end was considerable. The "Slippery" Tour comprised 200 shows and grossed $35M in ticket sales alone during the tour referred to as "the tour without end," and I was the guy who handled it for Doc. On top of that were record sales and merchandising, and Doc had a 20% commission on all of it. So I patiently waited for Doc to ask me to dinner and give me the check. When it didn't happen in Hawaii, I said, OK, it'll be when we get back and settle the books. But it didn't happen then either.

But while we were in Hawaii, I just enjoyed the time off with the company of my friends, not for a minute doubting that they would always have my back the way I always had theirs.

It was pure recreation for two weeks—THIS time far away from the Cayman Islands

Tico and Doc take the road to Hana—a remote village to the east

Dorothea and Jon in Hawaii at the end of the tour

Doc Gets Busted

On June 20, 1987, Jordan flew out from NY to Irvine, California to meet with Doc and Jon to pitch a concert idea he had for Bon Jovi to do a 20th anniversary of Woodstock concert at the Berlin Wall. The wall was definitely coming down, and it would be an indelible tribute to rock and roll if Bon Jovi was there when it happened. History books would remember

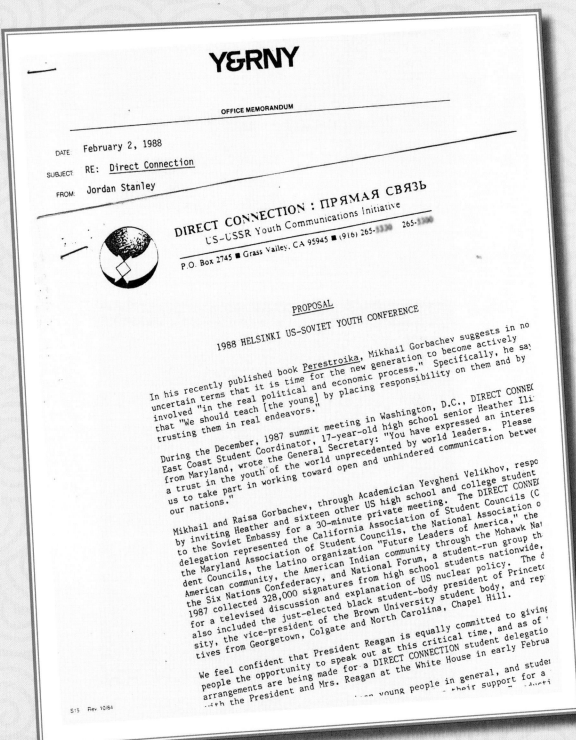

Y&RNY

OFFICE MEMORANDUM

DATE: February 2, 1988

SUBJECT: RE: Direct Connection

FROM: Jordan Stanley

DIRECT CONNECTION : ПРЯМАЯ СВЯЗЬ
US-USSR Youth Communications Initiative

P.O. Box 2745 ■ Grass Valley, CA 95945 ■ (916) 265-▮▮▮▮ 265-▮▮▮▮

PROPOSAL

1988 HELSINKI US-SOVIET YOUTH CONFERENCE

In his recently published book Perestroika, Mikhail Gorbachev suggests in no uncertain terms that it is time for the new generation to become actively involved "in the real political and economic process." Specifically, he say that "We should teach [the young] by placing responsibility on them and by trusting them in real endeavors."

During the December, 1987 summit meeting in Washington, D.C., DIRECT CONNEC East Coast Student Coordinator, 17-year-old high school senior Heather Ili· from Maryland, wrote the General Secretary: "You have expressed an interes a trust in the youth of the world unprecedented by world leaders. Please us to take part in working toward open and unhindered communication betwe our nations."

Mikhail and Raisa Gorbachev, through Academician Yevgheni Velikhov, respo by inviting Heather and sixteen other US high school and college student to the Soviet Embassy for a 30-minute private meeting. The DIRECT CONNEC delegation represented the California Association of Student Councils (C the Maryland Association of Student Councils, the National Association o dent Councils, the Latino organization "Future Leaders of America," the American community, the American Indian community through the Mohawk Na· the Six Nations Confederacy, and National Forum, a student-run group th· 1987 collected 328,000 signatures from high school students nationwide, for a televised discussion and explanation of US nuclear policy. The d also included the just-elected black student-body president of Princet· sity, the vice-president of the Brown University student body, and rep· tives from Georgetown, Colgate and North Carolina, Chapel Hill.

We feel confident that President Reagan is equally committed to givin people the opportunity to speak out at this critical time, and as of · arrangements are being made for a DIRECT CONNECTION student delegatio ·ith the President and Mrs. Reagan at the White House in early Februa
· ·· young people in general, and stude·
· their support for a ·

S15 Rev 10/84

how only rock and roll had the power to transcend culture and language barriers and unite the world through the youth of the world—anyway, why should the Pope and Reagan get all the credit? After all, if rock and roll proved anything, it was its universal appeal to the youth of the world—regardless of cultural background. It would be the perfect way to update the Woodstock spirit and put Bon Jovi on the 6 o'clock news. The truth is, even today, if you put together an audience of teenage Shiites, Sunnis, Jews, Hindus, Buddists, Palestinians, Saudis, Mexicans, Europeans, Japanese and Americans in the Coliseum with Bon Jovi, Jon would have them all rocking together like it was Woodstock in about 15 minutes! Back in 1987, the planned the "Berlin Wall" event was targeted to be something like that—the most significant concert event in the history of rock and roll, and there were almost two full years to prepare for it. Stanley began planning the event in cooperation with a youth group from the USSR called Direct Connection and the Vail Group in L.A.

However, after enthusiastically embracing the project, Doc went dark in February and couldn't be reached to draft the contract and next steps. In the interim, what had happened was that Doc was implicated in a drug conspiracy charge involving the smuggling of 20 tons of marijuana into Morehead City, North Carolina and pled guilty to the charge in federal court in NY on January 19. And on April 4, he was scheduled to be sentenced in U.S. District Court for the Eastern District of North Carolina. Doc was facing a tough judge and an aggressive prosecutor and could have been sentenced to 20 years or more for his role in the crime. But he had an ace-in-the-hole that he hoped would help him avert jail time completely. That was to do community service. Normally, community service is an option if you're 18 and get caught with a joint in your car. But getting caught with 20 tons of the shit is the equivalent of being pulled over with over 18,000,000 joints on you. You are going to jail.

But not Doc.

The official story is that some consultant came up with the idea that McGhee should stage rock concerts to raise money for drug-treatment programs instead of going to jail. But the idea of staging rock concerts to raise money for drug-treatment programs was actually Doc's idea, and he felt he had a better chance of the judge buying into it if he could recruit Jon Bon Jovi himself to make the case for him personally. Having more loyalty and allegiance to Doc than anyone else at that point for what he had done to advance his career, Jon sat down and wrote a letter directly to North Carolina District Court Judge W. Earl Britt making the case.

Here's the letter that Jon wrote to the presiding judge that persuaded him to let Doc off scot free without doing a single day of jail time:

Honorable W. Earl Britt
United States District Court
Eastern District
New Bern Division
Federal Building
310 New Bern Ave.
Raleigh, NC 27601

Your Honor,

My name is John Bongiovi, and I am the singer/songwriter of Bon Jovi, the band whom Doc McGhee manages.

I think that as we cannot meet face to face I should let you know a little bit about myself and my organization.

I am the eldest of three children, born and raised in Sayreville, New Jersey. My father and mother worked in the area, my dad as a hairdresser and my mom as a florist where we all pitched in to help whenever we could. You see, we are very family oriented. They have always supported my dream of becoming a quote "Rock Star."

They felt that if you believed in something and worked hard enough, there weren't any limitations. From the time I played my first talent show up to and through my signing with Polygram Records in 1983, it was all family. So what was most important to me in a real manager was not that he could get to a record company or a promoter on my behalf. He would have to be my brother and my best friend because I had to trust him not with a dollar or with my music, but literally with my life. A manager can always manage, a record company can always put out records, but as an artist it's only one shot.

If you trust someone and he directs you wrong or steals from you, it's as we say here in N.J., "back to Kinney" (the shoe chain).

I met Doc in June of '83 in NYC at a show at which several of the industry's top managers were courting me. One, David Krebs, had 26 platinum albums to his credit. John Scher, a NY/NJ promoter, had the offer of constant touring—always being able to go on the road which is important to a new band, and Stewart Young, an Englishman with offices in NY, LA and London managed bands like AC/DC and Billy Squier who I admired a lot. You may ask what then did Doc McGhee with no platinum albums, no promise of a tour and no other acts of prominence have to offer? Well it was his personality and his thoughts that I had something to offer the public. We were a band of kids playing for kids—to act as role models you might say. It was always Doc's concern that we didn't try to be something or someone we were not. We were just to have fun, and we didn't have to compete with other bands be it image wise

Jon's actual handwritten draft

Jon's actual handwritten draft

or musically. It was Doc who would be there not only for me or the band but any of the road crew or any and all of our families.

You see, your honor, Doc did in fact commit a crime, and I realize the severity of his case. But a man with his knowledge and commitment to the music industry can do so much good as a public servant.

The media exposure and severity of this case has in fact drawn attention to our organization. Many of my peers and all of my friends would sell their shirts for a chance to be managed by Doc.

I have also been informed about many of the long term community service ideas the attorneys have proposed, such as "live and type" concerts, print and even public service video and educational films, and I feel these can help to make a difference. Also, your honor, I would like to offer my services in any way to assist in the production as well as promotion of any of these concepts.

In closing, I'd like to say that as of April 30, 1988, my management contract expires with McGhee Entertainment and I have every intention of re-signing with Doc and his company with whom I enjoy working, and more importantly trust. If I can be of any assistance please feel free to contact me at any time.

Very respectfully yours,
John Bongiovi

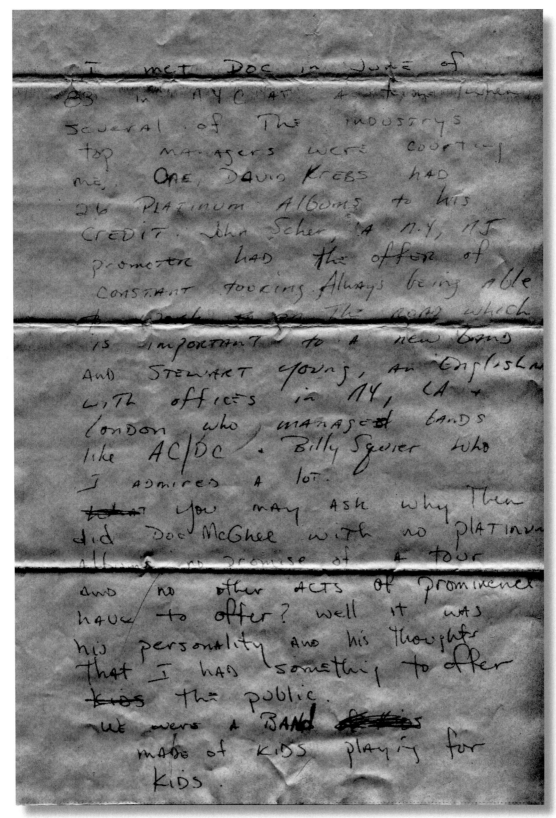

I met Doc in June of 83 in NYC at a time when several of the industry's top managers were courting me. One, David Krebs had 26 Platinum Albums to his credit. John Scher, a N.Y, N.J promoter had the offer of constant touring always being able to book the many which is important to a new band and Stewart Young, an Englishman with offices in NY, LA + London who managed bands like AC/DC. Billy Squier who I admired a lot.

You may ask why then did Doc McGhee with no Platinum Albums no promise of a tour and no other acts of prominence have to offer? well it was his personality and his thoughts that I had something to offer the public.

We were a BAND made of kids playing for kids.

Jon's actual handwritten draft

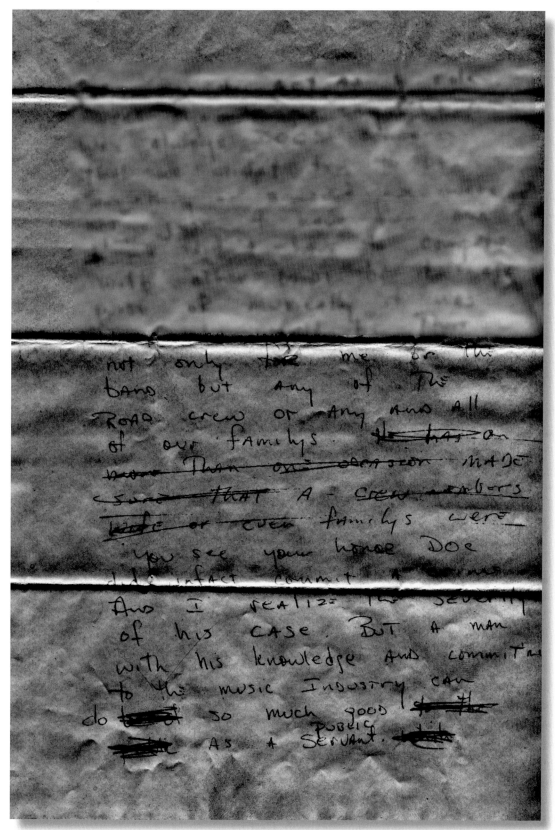

not only ~~the~~ me or the
band. but any of The
Road crew or any and all
of our familys ~~the~~ ~~has on~~
~~been Than on occasion~~ made
~~sure~~ ~~That~~ a ~~crew~~ ~~members~~
~~kids~~ or ~~even~~ familys were
you see your honor Doe
did infact commit ~~~~

And I realize the severity
of his case. But a man
with his knowledge and commitment
to the music Industry can
do ~~to get~~ so much good ~~for the~~
~~public~~ As a public Servant. ~~~~

Jon's actual handwritten draft

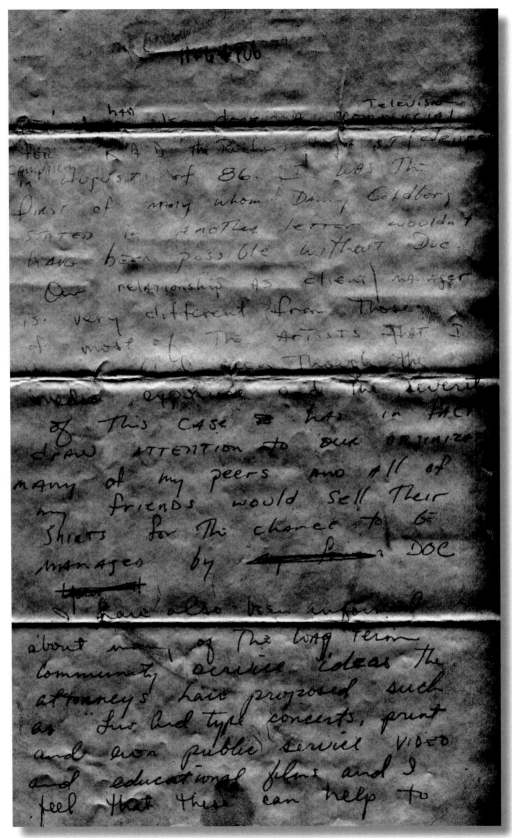

Jon's actual handwritten draft

Jon's actual handwritten draft

"Celebrity" has a powerful persuasive power. The judge went along with the proposal and that was the end of the "Berlin Wall" concert event and the beginning of the "Make a Difference Foundation." McGhee recruited Bon Jovi, Ozzy Osbourne, Mötley Crüe, the Scorpions and Skid Row to play what was billed as "The Moscow Peace Festival." It was positioned as an anti-drug concert, but most of the performers were completely zoned out on pot, pills and alcohol on the plane on the way over there. The only indication that this concert started off with the higher ambition of promoting world peace (thru rock and roll and the youth of the world) was that the word "peace" inexplicably remained in its title. But Doc did manage to get off the hook, and what's more got both of his bands involved in one event so he wouldn't have to fight about one band being in it and one band not being in it. As it turned out, "The Moscow Peace Festival" was the end of the road for Doc and Motley. Doc is said to have told Mötley they would be headlining and that no one would have any special effects. And when Bon Jovi opened up to a fairly theatrical entrance and opening with lots of pyro, Tommy Lee cold-cocked Doc and fired him on the spot. So much for keeping both bands happy.

As part of Doc's multi-year probation with the court, Bon Jovi played at a 1989 show at Broughton High School in Raleigh, and Doc raised money for an anti-drug documentary on MTV and a heavy metal album, Stairway to Heaven, Highway to Hell, but that was it.

All the band's efforts outside of touring were now going to be dedicated to the anti-drug message, and that effectively put an end to the bigger, enduring opportunity of positioning the band as the common denominator to youth of the world. But Doc had proven himself to be the smartest and most calculating manager anywhere—the Michael Corleone of rock.

It wasn't unusual for Jon to go to bat for someone who had done right for him, and there was nothing wrong about it. I'm sure he had the best of intentions. As you may recall, Jon had gone to bat for another McGhee employee, Art Voyeisk, when he was convicted of trafficking cocaine—because he tried to do right by those who had done right by him. He didn't have to do that, but to his credit,

"Doc" Corleone...

he did.

After "Slippery," we were all home for the holidays when I got the call from the chairman's office at "The American Music Awards." Bon Jovi had been nominated for favorite rock band, favorite rock album and favorite rock single. I was subtly advised that our seats were in the 3rd row and that our attendance was "mandatory" on January 25, 1988 in L.A., so we had a pretty good feeling we were going to win something. Patti and I and Jon and Dorothea "double-dated" that night. It was the best time we ever had. We all had worked hard for that recognition—

Glen Campbell and David Lee Roth about to announce Bon Jovi winner of "Favorite Rock Band" at American Music Awards

the band, crew, everyone—and it was particularly gratifying when the band's name was announced as the winner for favorite rock group and Jon and Richie went up to receive it.

It had been 4 years ago to the day that the band and I set out on the Runaway tour for the first time, and we had fulfilled and exceeded every one of our wildest dreams. After the awards ceremony, we were invited to a huge after-party at Grauman's Chinese Theatre. My most vivid memory of that night was pulling up in front of the spotlight-lit theatre with

Worst picture of Jon and Richie ever—as they hear the good news

Patti, me, Jon and Dorothea celebrate winning at Music Awards

throngs of fans swarming on either side. It was truly a surreal feeling walking from the limos to the front door. All the people were interesting and gracious, and most of them made a point of coming over to offer their congratulations. The festivities went on all night, and we had the chance to chat with just about everyone. At the time, Richie Sambora was dating Stacy Alden. But that night, it

was someone else who caught his eye—Cher. Richie was struck by her amazing presence, beauty and sophistication. She was truly in a league of her own, but as friendly and down-

to-earth as anyone you would hope to meet. Shortly afterwards, Richie would ask me to reach out to her agent and arrange for the two to meet. I did, and it blossomed into a very special and enduring romance.

For me, things were great, but I was starting to wonder what had become of the 5% stake in Bon Jovi that I was promised by Doc. After all, the band had achieved the superstardom it had sought, and I had done the job as well as it could be done. The "Slippery" tour had now been over for a couple months, but still no word from Doc. I started getting a little antsy but tried not to make my feelings show, because I didn't want to get Jon in the middle of my business with Doc.

Cher— timeless beauty, and Richie's future flame

DEAD PHOTOGRAPHER'S PICTURES SURFACE

Early in 1988, the photographer who took the aborted 1985 promotion pictures mysteriously died while away on vacation—setting in motion a blinding shit storm of fuckage.

A panic-stricken Jon Bon Jovi immediately called up Doc to tell him that we needed to track down the pictures as soon as possible. He told Doc there were more pictures taken during that session than either we or Polygram were aware of—including quite a few that were even more explicit. The photographer had held them back from Polygram on his own or at Jon's request so as to not shock or offend the staffers over there with photos they couldn't possibly use in the mainstream press.

By this time, Bon Jovi had achieved fame on a worldwide scale, so the guys felt they had a lot to lose personally and professionally if all or some of the photos ended up getting publicized. Jon in particular was concerned that some of them could undermine his all-American image and possibly jeopardize his musical career; his prospective movie career, or erode his corporate appeal for high-end endorsements. It was time to circle the wagons and get those pictures, and to do it fast, because the band had gotten so big that the damage would be impossible to control if they leaked out.

Doc instructed me to get a hold of the photos so that no one else could, so I called the photographer's office to track them down. The photographer's business partner, Greg*, told me that his office and belongings where inaccessible because they where tied up in probate. Greg said he would call the minute anything changed.

Normally I was able to get things done before anyone got a second chance to ask me whether I did them. But with the courts involved, I told Doc that it looked like it was going to take a while to get closure on this. Doc said that was unacceptable because "Jonny wanted answers right away." I told him that I fully understood the urgency of the request, but that everything was tied up in probate, and it was best to just wait until we got an "all-clear" from Greg. At that point I wasn't going to do anything that was illegal or could be construed as untoward for Doc or anyone else, because I had worked too hard for the band and didn't want to do anything

Doc wasn't happy that we couldn't get the pictures

that could make me a fall guy for Doc or anyone else. Doc didn't argue the point—but he clearly wasn't happy.

It took at least a week or two for Greg to call me back to say the probate had been concluded. But he said he managed to get in and look around for the photos, but couldn't find anything at all pertaining to Bon Jovi or any open Bon Jovi job. Upon hearing that, everyone's imagination started running wild. Where the fuck were the pictures? Which ones were sent to Polygram? Did Polygram send them back? Was his office burglarized? Did someone steal them? Who knew about them? How did they know? I didn't think things could get any worse, but they were just getting started.

I told Greg the pictures had to be there and asked him to make it a personal priority to find them, and to overnight them to me as soon as he located them. Then I posted Doc and went about my business. At that point, Doc got Julie Foley and Margaret Sterlacci from the office on the case and told them to aggressively track them down.

A week later, Doc invited me out for a round of golf. Just before I left, a FedEx package arrived from Greg. It was the pictures! They had been kept in a safe deposit box, and when the fee hadn't been paid after the photographer died, the bank returned the pictures to Greg, and Greg sent them to me. Man, was I excited. This was perfect. I would bring the pictures along to the golf course, surprise Doc with them, and use the occasion to settle the business of the 5% stake I had coming—all in the context of a round of golf. It couldn't have worked out better!

But as Doc greeted me at the golf course, he said he had some bad news. He said Jon was thinking about making a change, and I might be replaced! He said if I just walked away from Bon Jovi, he would give me a piece of Skid Row, right on the spot. I couldn't believe what I was hearing. Doc had promised me medical insurance, a pension, 5% piece of Bon Jovi, and now we're talking about me leaving Bon Jovi and starting all over again with Skid Row? What were the chances of Skid Row making it as big as Bon Jovi? And what were the chances I would actually get the 5% then if I didn't get what I earned now? This was way too much to hear all at once. And considering the fact that I was preparing for something very positive to have happened, I was caught completely by surprise.

Doc's word no longer meant anything to me. I had given him absolute allegiance and loyalty, and in return, he decided not to give me what he had promised and what I had earned. It was as though he was actually trying to get me so pissed-off I would just quit and walk away so he wouldn't have to give me anything. He didn't even cite any specific reason for Jon replacing me other than the fact that Jon was expecting to be doing larger venues on the New Jersey tour. But that made even less sense. There was no one more experienced than I was, plus I knew everything about the band and they were like my brothers. There's no way they could replace me with someone more qualified. None of it made any sense. It occurred to me that Doc was just trying to back out of giving me the percentage stake in Bon Jovi that he had promised me. I couldn't be sure if it was Jon who wanted me gone or whether it was just Doc orchestrating things to look that way. Surely Doc had a motive for getting rid of me—he didn't want to pay me what he promised. But I was speechless. I didn't know what to say or what to do. I certainly wasn't going to bring up the pictures at that point. That could wait until another day, a better time. Anyway, I figured that once Julie and Margaret found out that I had the pictures, they would tell Doc and he would have to talk about what I was promised then. It would be, "OK, you want the pictures, I want the 5% you promised me," and that would be that. Then I would get what I was promised, Jon would be happy, and Doc would be a hero in Jon's eyes—boom, everybody's happy. So I just stayed cool and waited for Doc to call me.

In the meantime, I started seeing a similar story playing out all around me. Just as the band had reached superstardom, Doc and the brain trust were trying to figure out how to avoid giving the hired help what they promised they'd get if the band made it. After all, it's easy to make promises when you don't have anything, but comes the time to deliver on those promises, and you have to take cash out of your pocket to do so, greed makes people do things they might not ordinarily do.

They started firing crew—people who like me had been around from the beginning; people who bet correctly on a million-to-one shot, but who were still going to lose anyway. They began replacing people with other people who had no expectations of health insurance, a 401K or any piece of the band because they had nothing to do with helping the band reach stardom. It's not like the crew felt that they should all get a piece of the band. But as people who went to work for the band when the band was unknown, and who worked their asses off and bled through the pores for the band and watched them like proud parents from the wings as they achieved stardom, the least they should have been given was whatever they were promised upfront and the right to continue to work with them.

But cutting them off would insure a bigger piece of the pie for the guys who owned the business rather than the guys running the business—primarily Doc.

Meanwhile, dissent was starting to brew inside the band. There were huge and unjustified differences in compensation between what Jon was earning and what the rest of the band was earning. Jon originally rationalized these differences based on the fact that he alone started the band. He alone made the first hit record. He alone got them their record deal. And indeed he was correct—all those things were true. The band would be nowhere without him.

But it was now 1987 and the band had reached the pinnacle of stardom. And they did it powered by the live performances of every member of the band. Unfortunately, Jon was locked-into a 4-year old point of view that was no longer relevant—and which no one had the courage or temerity to explain to him. This band was now undeniably powered by the live performances of every member in it. And the live performances of the band were powered by the management and crew and the infrastructure of Polygram and McGhee Entertainment. What really happened between the beginning of the "Slippery" tour and the end of the New Jersey tour was that the band members and management had become increasingly integral to the business, but their compensation didn't reflect that. This was a business tirelessly driven by live performance, and every one of the guys in the band was holding up his end and working as hard as the others for nearly 4 years now and as the realization starting sinking in—that not only were they each underpaid, but had been for the past several years—there was increasing distemper in the ranks. By the start of the New Jersey tour in 1988, and despite the success of the record, the exuberance was clearly dissipating.

By 1987 Bon Jovi was powered by the live performances of everyone in the group

Bon Jovi began disintegrating from the inside out because of the combined effect of crew and staff feeling like they'd been ripped-off by Doc, and the more innocent but damaging lack of recognition of everyone's contribution on Jon's part. Regardless of the causes, for a lot of people who helped build the Bon Jovi brand, it felt the same as a mugging in a shit neighborhood or a Wall Street pension rape in a better one.

Just as I was thinking things couldn't get any worse, all hell broke loose when I came home in mid-January to start the U.S. portion of the New Jersey tour. When I got home, Patti was gone. She left a note saying she moved in with her friend Elaine, and my heart sank to an all-time low.

I didn't know exactly where Elaine's house was, but I got in my car and headed down Deer Park Ave at 130 miles an hour looking for it in the brand new BMW Jon bought me as a gift for the "Slippery" tour. I drove up and down side streets trying to spot her car or a house that looked familiar. I was so depressed I came within milliseconds of driving that car right into a wall. If only she had been patient a little longer, I thought…

Band discontent at the beginning of the NJ Tour led to the wheels coming off by the end of it

But as it turned out, she had waited. She had tolerated months of isolation and loneliness while I was out on the road. And it wasn't just that. Patti was very close to Doc's wife Wendy—as well as Jon's fiancé Dorothea—and somehow, Patti had gotten the sense that the walls were closing in around Doc, and when—not if—he was indicted for cocaine or pot smuggling, I would be made the fall guy. Patti saw my undying loyalty to Doc as blind loyalty that would ultimately end with me, (and probably her) going to jail or getting killed, and she got out while she could. Patti's leaving took me completely by surprise; although today I have to say I should have seen it coming and done more to head it off. She didn't yet know how Doc planned to screw me. Maybe she would have hung around a bit longer. Maybe she would have gotten out sooner.

As for Doc, I was naïve. I was worried about getting what I had coming to me and losing my job. I'd come from a neighborhood

Patti with Jon during better days

where a man's word was his bond, and nothing was valued or honored more highly than loyalty. I now felt I was working in a far less honorable neighborhood, where nothing of honor was valued. In one crystal clear moment, I understood how Patti had to leave to save her life, leaving me to face whatever consequences lay ahead on my own. It was one more price I would pay for having been 100% dedicated to Bon Jovi.

I put the negatives away, waiting for Margaret or Julie to tell Doc I had them. That way, Doc would have to come to me instead of me chasing him around. It was my last hope.

I didn't have any way of viewing the negatives, and I actually didn't even see the pictures until 2009 when I started writing this book. Some were group shots, some with just Jon—including topless and bottomless photos, with a lot of "action" taking place. I can't say what the consequences of the pictures coming out 25 years ago would have been, but today, they seem tame by all standards. And publishing them today proves I had them and didn't try to hurt the band as everyone apparently thought—even when I was broke and destitute after leaving the band. Today, they tell a major story of my life, and prove my love for the band I had helped build, despite having been abandoned by it and cheated by Doc.

In a period of weeks, I went from the highest point of my life, to the lowest, feeling nothing but the void of Patti's absence, and the question of what I would do going forward—knowing I was on my own and I couldn't trust Doc. By the end of the New Jersey tour, Bon Jovi would have 16 months of concerts under their belt, I would be gone—thrown out in almost unbelievable fashion, and the band members would just go home without so much as saying goodbye; putting an unofficial end to the band. How it all went down for me is spelled out in the final chapter of this book.

At first, I don't think Jon minded that much. I believe he considered it an opportunity to launch a solo career. And at that time I think he actually preferred pursuing a solo career. But in my estimation, Jon hadn't anticipated the loss of energy and excitement that would result by going on as a solo act surrounded by passionless studio players. And after two years without the most exciting band in the world behind him, he would miss the raw energy enough to humble himself and reach out to the guys to put the band together again.

THE UNSUNG HEROES

They don't sing and nobody knows who they are. But without them there's no show, and take my word for it: the passion with which they do their job manifests itself a hundred ways in the performance of the band you love. They're the crew—the guys who take care of the stage, the sound, the lights, the equipment, the security, the wardrobe, the transportation and travel arrangements. They collect the money, watch the bank account and tune the guitars. They set up the show, they break it down, city to city, state to state, country to country all over the world so you can see your favorite band, Bon Jovi, perform live. They're the band's first true fans—the Unsung Heroes. Here's the main crew for the "Slippery When Wet" Tour:

CREW PERSONNEL

John Hugdahl	Production Manager
Ralf Ambrosius	House Sound Engineer
Dave Davidian	Lighting Director
Jeff Tarbell	Band Technician
Gary Douglas	Band Technician
Dana Roun	Band Technician
Dave Stern	Band Technician
Steve Lemon	Rigger
Clay Carter	Ground Rigger
Nancy Spencer	Wardrobe
Curt Anthony	Pyrotechnician
Al Larson	Carpenter
Paul Loret	Carpenter
Ian McFarland	Starlights
Roger Gibbons	Starlights
Laurie Quigley	Sound
Bill Chrysler	Sound
Arthur Kemish	Sound
Jeff Williams	Sound
Francois Demartini	Sound
Mark Coleman	Lights
Steve Harris	Lights
Mick McGuire	Lights
Jeff Mateer	Lights
George Harvey	Lights
Joe Mullin	Bus Driver
Doyle Nelson	Bus Driver
Don Register	Bus Driver
Jim Freuck	Truck Driver
Randy Rhodes	Truck Driver
Keith Stuckey	Truck Driver
J.R.Loret	Truck Driver
Dave Gist	Truck Driver
Charlie Bisbing	Truck Driver
Jeff Hamer	Merchandising
Doug Gall	Merchandising

"Slippery When Wet" Band and crew—a once-in-a-lifetime combination of talent and dedication

A lot is said about the support of family and friends. And of course I only have good things to say about supportive people. But it's the crew members who actually believe in the band and sacrifice gainful employment elsewhere in exchange for minimum wage. They give up their families, friends and girlfriends to be with the band on the road because they truly believe in them and want to be a part of the long-shot of actually helping them achieving stardom. They will bet wrong 95% of the time. And only a fraction of the remaining 5% who survive the first year will actually be there for a second year. And only a fraction of those who survive that will achieve stardom. So just try hitching your wagon to a star. The only way you take on odds like that is by working for a band you believe in.

David with his keyboard tech Dave Stern

My dad, Robert Bozzett and wardrobe person, Nancy Spencer

The tough part is that in those rare instances when a band actually does make it, one of the first thing that typically happens is the band hires more accountants and lawyers to watch over their ever-increasing revenue streams and costs; and those son-of-a-bitches replace the original crew with cheap labor just as they are getting to the point where they have to give them or pay them what they promised when they were just starting out.

Why on earth would a band ever let go of people whose loyalty and commitment could never be questioned? The only answer is "greed"—and to me, that kind of greed isn't just stupid because it erodes the organization, it's just plain sacrilegious. But it happens all the time. OK, so a guy takes a job and it doesn't work out. That's a sad thing but not necessarily a bad thing. It's part of life. Many people walk through the same fire in a million different professions. You roll the dice and hope for the best, no guarantees. If it doesn't work out, it's not necessarily someone's fault. But when the band makes it big and everybody doesn't come along and get a taste, it's just wrong. Hey, those guys bet correctly on a million-to-one shot. To have it taken away isn't "business" —it's dishonorable. Anyone can find someone who will do the same job cheaper

Kevin O'Brien (lighting director); Rick Lawrence (stage mgr); Jeff Tarbell (drum tech) and Gary Douglas (guitar technician)

once a band is famous. It's now proven, gainful employment. What's the bet? And what did the guy who came on after the band made it contribute to the band?

It's not just a simple quest to find cheap labor; it's just a way of evading the responsibility of giving people what they were promised. But these folks weren't just doing a "job." They were working away from home, living with a different family with lots of habits that aren't particularly conducive to having a stronger bond at home. So they should do better than the average Joe in the average job. But they don't. And sure these guys could get work again, but probably with a new opening act. And who in their right mind would bet twice on the same situation with a different band—assuming they were lucky enough to find another band to believe in, and lucky enough for the band to make it—who's to say the exact thing wouldn't happen exactly the same way again? So there they are, screwed. And assuming you had enough money to pay a lawyer for his advice at every turn, no amount of lawyered paperwork is going to save you if it's your boss' intention to screw you.

Security detail Danny Francis and Bill Greer between Jon and Tico

Crew people should be exalted by their bands—because their belief enables others to believe.

I made the transition back to civilian life.

But I'm sure there are many more like me who were thrown under the bus before their promises came to fruition who weren't able to make the transition back to civilian life. They are truly unsung heroes. They put aside their families and other job opportunities to work 24 hours a day, 7 days a week to help 5 guys achieve their dreams of stardom—then they watched from the wings with pride as they did it.

My band and crew were like real family to me. We lived together and did everything together for years at a time. They were there from the beginning, and once you achieve fame you really can't look at any of the people you meet and trust them the same way ever again. When you see them discarded like Kleenex because there's no place on a balance sheet that shows that the guy you just canned worked for 2 years for minimum wage and bled through the pores before the band made it, and only wanted what was promised to him. But they are cut loose without a thought because the audience will never miss them. That's a scumbag cowardly move, and I hope the folks who did it earn a special trip to hell.

All too often, these guys end up on drugs, penniless, before they even know what hit them—or muttering to themselves in a psych ward. My best friend and mentor, Richie Fisher, my closest friend from childhood who lived four doors down from me and who became Mötley Crüe's tour manager and took them everywhere in the world, ended up broke, penniless and in a psych ward after

Richie Fisher was my best friend and mentor

No one ever even called Barry Ambrosio

trying to commit suicide by jumping off the famed Waldorf Astoria Hotel.

When former Bon Jovi guitar tech Barry Ambrosio got cancer, a family friend tried to reach out to the Bon Jovi organization to marshal some comfort and emotional support, but no one called him back, and there is a high probability no one in the band even got the message, and Barry died feeling abandoned.

Many more never got health insurance or a pension even though Doc used to represent to everyone who came into the office how he had put together a hell of a pension and medical package for all his employees. That was Doc at his bullshit best. In the very early days working for Doc as Pat Travers' valet, I was just dropped off the tour when I came down with pneumonia. Thankfully, someone where I was staying saw how badly I was doing and sent me to the hospital. I was later told if I hadn't gone when I did I would have died. Then I ended up with a $5000 hospital bill that I had to pay out of my own pocket. So just for the record, none one gave a shit about me when I was sick, much less took care of me or paid my bills. I was on my own.

Nobody wants or expects a free ride. After being dumped like yesterday's garbage these folks try to reinvent themselves despite the disillusionment and abandonment. But it's especially hard to get kicked out of your band because it feels like you're being kicked out of your family. And this has happened to hundreds of guys (and some gals), maybe thousands. I find it strangely hypocritical to see how big stars adopt charitable efforts as a tax shelter or public relations ploy, yet fail to think charitably about their own people.

With half of my proceeds from this book, I am starting the Unsung Heroes' Foundation—a charitable organization designed to find these guys, people like Richie, before they end up in a psych ward—and help them get back on their feet, access drug rehabilitation and get a fair pension or retirement in those cases where their bands achieved their dreams. In a way, it's a way of saving myself. If you've ever seen any Bon Jovi live show, or any live show, go to UnsungHeroesFoundation.net to learn more or to make a donation.

THE END

The end for me came after a night of partying in Houston on the New Jersey tour. Richie Sambora, David Bryan and I were out hitting strip clubs until about 1 AM. It was February 9, 1989. When we returned to the hotel and hung out with Richie until 4 or 5 AM. When we returned to the hotel, Richie told me Jon was furious with me, although he didn't know why. He told me I needed to be on my toes because the end could be at hand. Richie asked if I did anything wrong. I said, "No," and I was confused too. Whatever it was that happened, he must have found out about it after we got back to the hotel and he returned to his room because he never mentioned it while we were out.

Taking the band across Japan during the "Slippery When Wet" tour

Two days later we were in Puerto Rico and after the show I was waiting for Jon to meet me in the hotel lobby to fly back to Miami when Doc came down instead.

Doc told me that one of the secretaries from our main office found out that the fabled pictures from the aborted 1985 promotion had been sent to me—but instead of calling Doc to tell him, she left a message at the hotel that Jon picked up instead. I was in shock. I think she called while we were still in Houston, and Jon asked her for confirmation that the pictures were sent to me, which he got while we were in Puerto Rico. That would explain why Jon was suddenly furious in Houston, and why the whole episode blew up two days later. I told Doc that I thought the secretary would call Doc and that Doc would come to me and we would resolve all our business without anyone else getting involved.

Needless to say, my grand plan for bringing Doc back to the table to tie off the business between us had just blown up in my face. I should have known I really didn't have a chance against Doc. Now, instead of using the photos to get what I had coming from Doc in exchange for making him look like a hero for delivering the pictures to Jon, I ended up on Jon's shitlist for keeping pictures that he perceived as a threat to him and the band. It was a blinding shit storm of fuckage. Not only did my "grand plan" for getting what I was promised backfire and put me on the defensive with Jon, it gave Doc all the ammunition he would need to be able to fire me (and not give me my percentage) without Jon objecting to it! Nice work, Rich. But I was still going to get the chance to air the whole issue out with Doc and Jon, so I trusted everything would still work out and everything would be OK.

We rented two private Learjet's to fly back to Miami—one for just Jon, me and Doc, the other for the rest of the band, crew and everybody else. On the flight back with just the three of us, I thought everything could be talked through and resolved. But that was not to be the case.

By the time our plane took off, it was well after midnight on the 11th and we were all tired. As the three of us sat down, Doc started the discussion by telling me that Jon was furious because I didn't tell him that I had the pictures. But Doc knew damn well that I was pissed off because he had not yet given me the percentage of the band he had promised. Doc also knew at that point that I had intended for him to find out I had the pictures and come to me to get them. For months he just kept evading the issue and doing everything he could to put it off, perhaps thinking that doing so would wear me down and get me used to the idea of not getting it. But I had worked far too hard and given up far too much to drop the issue or let him off the hook. So my response was, "Damn right I have them, where's the 5% I was promised?"

Jon responded, "I didn't promise you 5%," to which I said, "No, he did," pointing at Doc. Doc knew better than to deny what he had told me right to my face, so he didn't acknowledge the point. He was on the winning end if he could keep this about me and Jon instead of about me and him. I guess that was easy to do because Jon was already angry with me.

But at that point, I expected Jon to weigh in and say to Doc, "Look, if you promised that to him, you should give it to him." But he didn't say anything. I felt totally abandoned. I had taken a lot of bullets for Jon. I even lost my fiancé over the band. But when the time came for him to have my back, he sat in silence.

Doc said, "Rich, look, you're burnt out from being on the road, I want you to work out of the office now." Doc was the master of bullshit. With one response, he appeared to be disciplining me in front of Jon by taking me off the road, and telling me this wasn't the time or place to resolve my percentage, but not to worry because I'll still be working for McGhee Entertainment and we'd sort it out later. But I found out he was full of shit two weeks later when I went to work at the office as planned and there was no job there for me when I arrived. When he said it on the plane, I figured he'd have to be telling the truth because he said it in front of Jon.

So Doc had managed to outsmart both of us. He didn't come clean in front of Jon about my motive for having the pictures, and he didn't give me the percentage of the band I had earned. It was really that simple. It didn't matter what I had given up or done for the band, or what pieces of me were scattered on the side of the road from the past six years. I already did the work and he already had the money I had earned for him. So the way he looked at it, what was the point of paying me?

So there we were—all of us exhausted, and Jon and I were in such a state that neither of us were able to articulate anything that made any sense, much less listen to each other. For the last 45 minutes of the flight, no one had anything to say.

Still, there were two things that didn't square up. If my having the pictures was considered so serious a problem to have me fired, wouldn't firing me actually encourage me to run right out and publish the pictures? And if they knew that I had no intention of publishing the pictures, why would it be considered so serious an offense that they would fire me? Even though Doc managed to outsmart both Jon and me, neither Jon nor Doc seemed to have one clear-thinking mind between the two of them.

But in the days ahead, they began playing me as if I was a danger to the band. Once again, Doc reassured me that even though I was coming off the road, I'd still be working out of the home office on Bon Jovi, and told me to come in two weeks to get started.

Then they ran Bon Jovi business manager Bruce Kolbrenner at me to reiterate that I had still had my health insurance and pension coming.

Then Jon asked to meet with me in the city, at which time he asked me to just burn the pictures. Jon had every reason to expect that I would because he could always count on me to do as he wanted. But at that point, I had been repeatedly screwed over and I wasn't working for him or being paid by him any more. So I had no obligation to do what I was asked, and every reason not to. I let everyone believe the pictures were destroyed just to see what would happen. Once they were convinced the pictures were gone, it was every asshole for himself.

Rock and roll's equivalent of a gold watch

No one followed up on a single promise they made. They were all full of shit.

There was never any follow-up from Bruce regarding a pension or health insurance. When I went in to work at Doc's office, he said he didn't have a job for me after all, which left me so completely numb, I just walked out the door speechless. And of course, Doc would never call to pay me the 5% he owed me. After he thought the pictures were destroyed, I didn't exist.

I would see Jon a month after I was fired and five more times over the next several years. Once he called me to tell me his little brother Tony was nabbed at the Mexican border for allegedly smuggling cocaine; once he stopped by my house while I was out; and again, he called to invite me to his wedding. But incredibly, Jon never explained why I was fired, nor did he try to reach out and make amends for what was done to me because, technically, I wasn't his responsibility. He was paying big dollars to Doc for Doc to take care of me.

Well it wasn't long before Doc was gone too. And that breakup was even more acrimonious. I think the catalyst for Doc getting fired was Jon's feeling that Doc didn't have a real commitment to the "Make a Difference Foundation." That, and the fact that Jon needed to prove to himself that he could still be Jon without having Doc around--a daunting task, because regardless of how Doc treated me, he was, and still is, the most calculating, creative and ruthless manager out there. That's why everybody wants him.

Soon after that, Bruce Kolbrenner was gone. Then more crew… They were dropping like flies. I was the first domino to fall. But by the end of the tour, *everyone* was gone, including the band! The way I heard it, they just split in different directions without even saying goodbye.

Each one of those guys has had 20 years to reach out to me and do the right thing. But once they thought I wouldn't make their life difficult, they chose to abandon me the same way they abandoned everyone that Jon would ever have to admit played a pivotal role in his success. As for me, I was back home, right where I started. I took a job with a landscaper named Romanzi digging post holes in rocky loam to set fence posts. Yes, the same hands that helped build one of the biggest bands in the world were now bleeding and calloused from manual labor at $10 an hour.

After working there for nearly two months, the owner comped me two Giants tickets, way up in the nosebleed section. They were the second row from the top, but they were fine for me. On game day, guess who arrived by helicopter to play the halftime show. Yep, it was Bon Jovi, arriving in the same helicopter I'd flown in with them to this very arena. And the very helicopter I used to fly in with Jon was now passing so close over my head that I could almost touch it by standing up as it flew over the crest of the stadium and down to the field below.

When the band went on at halftime, the sound system wasn't working. Just as it had not worked at Madison Square Garden when Bon Jovi opened for ZZ Top twenty years ago to the day! Only this time, I was saddened in my heart that I wasn't able to help him get it fixed, put a smile on his face or reassure him in any way. This time Jon and the band would be on their own. I hadn't fully accepted the fact that I was fired until that moment. But somehow, the two mirror images of the Garden and the Stadium glaring in my mind represented to me a tangible beginning and end.

I had survived the most improbable journey from being a loader for a Columbian pot smuggling operation, to working for the biggest cocaine and pot smugglers in and out of the rock and roll business, to managing the tours of the biggest band of its time—without getting killed, arrested or going to jail. But I lost my fiancé, my job, my percentage of the band, my prospects of having health insurance, a pension, working out of the home office and my brotherhood with each of the guys in the band—all for no reason other than to avoid giving me what I had earned. I stood within the smallest circle of the biggest rock band of its time—from its first gig in obscurity, to the highest point of its collective career—and I saw how one man could "will" himself into superstardom. I watched Doc concoct a method of getting away with smuggling 20 tons of pot while thousands of users of those same 20 tons did, and are still doing, hard time for using it. And I'd seen Jon Bon Jovi climb to the top of the pop world on the backs of dozens of people who he shouldn't have allowed his accountants, lawyers and managers to throw under the bus.

As for the pictures, I surely paid for them. But I never even saw them until I started writing this book—the negatives sat in a safe deposit box for 25 years. And when I finally processed the negatives and saw all 4 rolls of pictures that were sent to me I couldn't understand why Jon and Doc were so upset. Granted there are a few R-rated ones, but nothing scandalous enough to pose a threat to anyone's career. At least not *today*.

Since then, I've heard Jon proclaim himself to be the CEO of his own brand, and I just shake my head. It's possible Jon won't ever be happy until he erases the memory of everyone and anyone who has ever helped him in his rise to stardom.

I lost heart in the business because I figured if I hadn't been able to earn health insurance or a pension from everything I did for Bon Jovi, I wouldn't get it from anybody else. Hell, these were my brothers and I was with them every step of the way, from their first gig to superstardom. If that can't get you health insurance, a pension or a piece of a band, nothing can.

Then I got a call from Sharon Osbourne who was managing Lita Ford as well as Ozzy. I had met her years before when Lita Ford opened for Bon Jovi in Europe. She invited me to come out to her house and talk about taking a tour manager job for her. She sent me a ticket and arranged for a car on the other end. We showed up at the front door; it was a very friendly and accommodating Ozzy who answered the door, invited me in and offered

to get me a drink. Sharon looked spectacular, and she too was gracious and accommodating. She had a way of making people feel special, no matter who they were. Sharon offered me a headlining tour manager rate to take out Lita Ford who was opening for Ozzy Osbourne, for which I was extremely happy and grateful. And of course I took the job. But at the end, when I had the chance to discuss going out with Ozzy on his tour, I couldn't imagine staying on the road as a long-term career. It's a young man's sport. After as many years as I had spent on the road, it seemed to me that tour managers should at some point end up back in the home office, taking care of business there instead of staying on the road for too long.

So in the end, I was back somewhere near the beginning. I spent a few months getting used to the idea of not being with Bon

The gorgeous and abundantly talented Lita Ford

Jovi, trying to figure out what to do to make a living. Desperate and destitute, I took a job scrubbing toilets at a construction site. It was quite a fall from grace—one minute you're touring the world with one of the most popular bands in the history of rock and roll, and the next minute, you're cleaning up shit at a construction site to avoid being homeless and having to sleep in the park.

Before too long I learned some trades and started teaching myself the construction business, ultimately starting a construction company of my own. But there was and would always be the mental pain. I would always be associated with Bon Jovi by everyone I knew. But I wasn't with the band anymore so I could never escape its memory. And I couldn't get over the pain of how it ended—it was a summary execution. No sit-down to tell my side, no "thank you's," no plaque or honorarium, no roast and no blindfold or last cigarette. In the end it was a quick shot behind the ear that took me out, and I never even heard it coming. I underestimated what greed makes people do. I sure didn't expect anyone to screw me over if I was doing a good job.

One night during the early days of "Slippery When Wet", I remember Richie turning to my dad as he was checking out the sound system for that night's show and he said, "Mr. B, we're going to be big, and your son is always going to be with us." Despite an unwavering loyalty to Doc that could have gotten me killed or landed me behind bars, and a complete commitment to Jon and Bon Jovi that cost me my fiancé and everything else I valued, it was surprisingly easy for Doc and Jon to send me packing instead of giving me what I was promised.

Recently, Patti reached out to me after not seeing or speaking to me in over 20 years. She was the one who chronicled my whole story in pictures. Whenever she was around, you could hear the camera clicking away as a remembrance of the most exciting time of our lives. Hundreds of her pictures are in this book. Best of all, in getting together to reminisce over the "birth" of the Bon Jovi band and its rise to superstardom, in some ways, it's like she never left, and a special friendship

Jon's bedroom and Superman poster

endures based on our having shared an extraordinary life experience that we both know is impossible to describe. Who knows where life will go for the two of us from here? But for the first time in 25 years, I do feel at peace.

In his Rumson house, Jon had a Superman poster next to his bed. He also has a Superman insignia on his left arm right below the shoulder. Jon aspires to be Superman, the guy who does it all. But he's constantly haunted by the fact that other songwriters, his management, band and support staff played a big role in getting him where he got. It's almost as though he will always need to see himself as being more than Jon Bon Jovi to be satisfied with being Jon Bon Jovi. In some irrational way, I think he considers what everyone else did to allow him to concentrate on being a star totally incidental to what he did to become one. But I don't believe any of the players in this epic ascent to superstardom were "incidental." In fact, looking at what was accomplished by everyone together, the only conclusion a rational person could come to is that every single person performed over and above, and each one of them was indispensible.

When a person has the ambition of a Jon Bon Jovi, it's hard to question the psychology driving him, because no doubt, he is capable of doing just about anything. But it is a psychology that values himself in the here-and-now more than any person who helped him in his time of need to get to the here-and-now…during a time so long ago.

Jon got the band together again in 1992 with the Keep the Faith album. That album debuted at #1 in both UK and Australia and reached Double Platinum status. In the US, it produced the Top 10 hit "Bed of Roses" while the title track hit number one.

In 1994, Bon Jovi released a 'greatest hits' album with two new tracks, titled Cross Road, which was the best selling album in UK for 1994. The first single off the compilation, "Always", spent six months on the top 10 of the Billboard Hot 100, certified platinum in the US and became Bon Jovi's highest selling single.

The band released their sixth studio album, These Days, a year later in 1995. These Days was a huge commercial success, especially in the Asian and European markets. The album debuted at #1 in UK where it replaced Michael Jackson's album HIStory at number one on the UK Albums Chart and spent four consecutive weeks at #1.

Bon Jovi returned in 2000 and released their seventh studio album, Crush. It became the band's sixth and fifth consecutive number one album in Australia and the United Kingdom, respectively, and reached double platinum in the US. The success of the album was largely due to the lead single "It's My Life" which was nominated for a Grammy Award for Best Rock Performance by a Duo or Group.

The band soon returned with an eighth studio effort in 2002, Bounce. It debuted at number two on the Billboard 200, making it Bon Jovi's highest debut in the band's 20-year history. This record was beaten, however, with the band's ninth studio album Have a Nice Day in 2005.

The band's tenth studio album, Lost Highway, was released in 2007. The album became the first Bon Jovi album to debut at number one in the US, making it the band's first number one in their home country since "Slippery When Wet".

The band returned to their rock roots in 2009 with their eleventh studio album, The Circle. The album also debuted at number one on the Billboard Hot 100, making it the band's fourth number one in the US.

According to Wikipedia, the discography of American rock band Bon Jovi consists of eleven studio albums, three compilation albums, one live album, one box set, thirteen video releases and over 50 singles, not including solo efforts of Jon Bon Jovi, Richie Sambora and David Bryan.

Till this day, when a Bon Jovi song comes on the radio I get warm feeling inside. But when I hear "Bad Name", "Wanted Dead or Alive" or "Living on a Prayer", I am instantly transported to the time and place where together we built the foundation for it all. A time and place that was like no other in the annals of rock history, and is not likely to ever be repeated.

Stacy, Wendy, Doc, Dorothea, me, Richie S., Alec, Jon (behind Alec), April and David

Index

PICTURE CREDITS

Ebet Roberts: pages 1, 73A, 139A.

Power Station Studio staff: page 2.

Patti O'Connor: pages 3-9, 15-16, 21, 27, 38-39, 57-60, 63, 68, 71, 80, 82, 85, 87, 110-112, 115, 127-128, 130, 139B, 140A, 142-147, 152.

Richard Bozzett: pages 10-11, 22, 23B-26, 28-31, 32B-34, 36-37, 40, 41, 42, 48, 55-56, 65, 70, 72, 73B-73C, 81, 83-84, 86, 93, 104-106, 113-114, 126, 134B, 150.

Steve Grennaldo: page 46.

Ron Akiyama: pages 13, 100-102, 133-134A, 137.

Tami Langan/LGI: pages 14, 17-20, 49-51, 140B.

Koh Hasebe: pages 23A, 78-79, 92, 94-98.

June Lanford: page 32A.

Ross Halfin: pages 35, 103.

New York Times February 7, 1985: page 54.

Paul Natkin/Photo Reserve Inc: pages 61-62, 107, 141.

© 1985 Motley Crue: page 69.

© Newsday February 9, 1986: pages 74, 76.

Bon Jovi, "Slippery When Wet" tour book: pages 88-91.

Sam Emerson MJJ Productions: pages 108-109.